THE AU

ROBERT D. LEIGH, di Commission on Freedom of the Press, is a well-known political scientist and for fourteen years was president of Bennington College. In the early part of World War II he acted as special adviser to the National Resources Planning Board. Later he became director of the Foreign Intelligence Broadcast Service of the Federal Communications Commission and chairman of the United Nations Monitoring Committee. Mr. Leigh is now a Visiting Professor of Political Science at the University of Chicago.

LLEWELLYN WHITE, assistant director of the Commission on Freedom of the Press, has had twenty-nine years of association with the press. His career has included work as copy chief of the *New York Herald Tribune*, assistant managing editor of the *Literary Digest*, national affairs director of *Newsweek*, and editor of the editorial pages and Washington correspondent of the *Chicago Sun*, in addition to work with A.P. and U.P. During the war he served in the New York branch of the Office of War Information, and immediately prior to his activity on the Commission on Freedom of the Press he worked with Elmer Davis on a program which would allow the O.W.I. to withdraw as private press agencies return to business in foreign countries formerly cut off by the war.

THE COMMISSION ON FREEDOM OF THE PRESS

ROBERT M. HUTCHINS, *Chairman*
Chancellor, University of Chicago

ZECHARIAH CHAFEE, JR., *Vice-Chairman*
Professor of Law, Harvard University

JOHN M. CLARK
Professor of Economics, Columbia University

JOHN DICKINSON
General Counsel, Pennsylvania Railroad

WILLIAM E. HOCKING
Professor of Philosophy, Emeritus, Harvard University

HAROLD D. LASSWELL
Director, War Communications Research, Washington, D.C.

ARCHIBALD MacLEISH
Formerly Assistant Secretary of State

CHARLES E. MERRIAM
Professor of Political Science, Emeritus, University of Chicago

REINHOLD NIEBUHR
Professor of Ethics and Philosophy of Religion, Union Theological Seminary

ROBERT REDFIELD
Dean, Division of the Social Sciences, University of Chicago

BEARDSLEY RUML
Chairman, Federal Reserve Bank of New York

ARTHUR M. SCHLESINGER
Professor of History, Harvard University

GEORGE N. SHUSTER
President, Hunter College

FOREIGN ADVISERS

JOHN GRIERSON
Former General Manager, Wartime Information Board, Canada

HU SHIH
Former Chinese Ambassador to the United States

*JACQUES MARITAIN
President, Free French School for Advanced Studies

KURT RIEZLER
Professor of Philosophy, New School for Social Research

STAFF OF THE COMMISSION

ROBERT D. LEIGH, *Director*
LLEWELLYN WHITE, *Assistant Director*
RUTH A. INGLIS
MILTON D. STEWART

* M. Maritain resigned February, 1945, to become French ambassador to the Holy See.

LLEWELLYN WHITE & ROBERT D. LEIGH

PEOPLES *SPEAKING TO* PEOPLES

A Report on International Mass Communication from The Commission on Freedom of the Press

THE UNIVERSITY OF CHICAGO PRESS · CHICAGO

The Commission on Freedom of the Press was created to consider the freedom, functions, and responsibilities of the major agencies of mass communication in our time: newspapers, radio, motion pictures, news-gathering media, magazines, books.

The Commission is operating under a grant of funds made by Time, Inc., to the University of Chicago. The University administers the funds, but neither it nor the donor has any jurisdiction over the Commission, which is a nongovernment, independent group containing no members of the press, radio, or motion-picture industries.

The general report of the Commission on Freedom of the Press will appear at the termination of its work. Meanwhile, however, the Commission will publish special studies. The present study in the field of international communication was prepared by Mr. White and Mr. Leigh of the Commission staff. It is published at this time because of the pressing urgency of certain problems in this field—specifically the problem of the participation of the government of the United States in peacetime international communication and information services. For the same reason the Commission publishes herewith its general recommendations with reference to international communication. The Commission does not undertake at this time to pass upon the specific proposals of Mr. White and Mr. Leigh for implementing the general recommendations but presents them for public discussion and the serious consideration of the persons and agencies framing policy in this field.

The University of Chicago Press · Chicago 37
Agent: Cambridge University Press · London

 Published 1946. Composed and printed by The University of Chicago Press, Chicago, Illinois, U.S.A.

STATEMENT BY THE COMMISSION

RECENT improvements in the machinery and methods of international communication have made possible, for the first time in history, direct communication across national boundaries to the masses of the people of the world. These mechanical improvements offer at once a new hope and a new danger. The choice is not between the use or the neglect of these new instruments of communication. The instruments exist and will be used in any case. The choice is between their full, purposeful, and responsible use to enlarge the mutual comprehension of peoples, on the one hand, and, on the other, their incomplete, undirected, and irresponsible use, with the risk of an increase in international hatred and suspicion as a consequence.

If they are used to the limits of their potentialities to increase the nations' knowledge of one another's character and purposes, they will enlarge the area of international understanding and enhance the hope of peace. If they are not so used, these innovations will merely serve to give wider international currency and more rapid dissemination to reports which may increase the distortion and misrepresentation of national conduct, character, and purpose, which have bred wars in the past.

We believe that attempts to suppress the presentation of evils and sources of conflict would be self-defeating. We believe that the cure for distorted information is more information, not less, because we believe the elements of common decency, humanity, and good will are strong enough to outweigh opposing elements if included in a comprehensive and representative picture.

In the opinion of the Commission, it is essential to the realization of our generation's hope for peace that prompt action be taken by governments and those responsible for the management of the international communication industries, to insure the full and considered use of these improved instruments of mass communication for enlarging the area of mutual comprehension between the peoples of the world. Such action would include:

a) The improvement of physical facilities and operating mechanisms so as to bring about the communication of words and images across national borders as abundantly, as cheaply, as quickly, as efficiently, and over as wide an area as possible;
b) The progressive removal of political barriers and the lessening of economic restrictions which impede the free flow of information across national borders; and
c) The improvement of the accuracy, representative character, and quality of the words and images transmitted in international communicaton.

As regards the role of the United States and its citizens in international communication between peoples, the Commission offers the following general recommendations:

1. The government and people of the United States should recognize the importance of a mutual understanding, as between peoples, of each other's true character and purposes and should be prepared not only to communicate to others a truthful and comprehensive account of our own national life and purposes but to receive and to circulate in the same spirit reciprocal communications with regard to other nations and peoples.

2. So far as the communication to the peoples of other nations of accounts of our own life and purposes is concerned, private industry should be looked to in ordinary course to disseminate through commercial channels the words and images necessary to a truthful and comprehensive representation.

3. It must, however, be recognized that such considerations as undue emphasis on commercially marketable words and images or the absence of profitable markets in certain parts of the world

may interfere with the ability of private industry to achieve in all cases the dissemination through commercial channels of a balanced and comprehensive representation of the United States and its people. A committee representing government and the management of the international communications industries should, therefore, be established at an early moment to provide for supplementary dissemination to areas, or under circumstances, in which commercial dissemination of an adequate representation of the American people is not feasible or cannot, for any reason, be expected.

4. This committee should attempt, in the first instance, to secure the required supplementary dissemination of words and images by inviting the participation of private industry on a noncommercial (i.e., public service) basis or through the agency of nonprofit societies, corporations, or foundations existing or to be established for the purpose.

5. Failing the provision of the required service by these means, the committee should request government, which should be adequately staffed and prepared for the purpose, to undertake the dissemination needed.

Robert M. Hutchins
Zechariah Chafee, Jr.
John M. Clark
John Dickinson
William E. Hocking
Harold D. Lasswell
Archibald MacLeish
Charles E. Merriam
Reinhold Niebuhr
Robert Redfield
Beardsley Ruml
Arthur M. Schlesinger
George N. Shuster

TABLE OF CONTENTS

1. The Problem 1

2. The Objective 13

3. The Physical Instruments 17

4. Merchants of Words and Images 56

5. The Hardest Job—Quality 84

6. Proposals 105

Note on Sources 113

Publications of the Commission 119

1

THE PROBLEM

CO-OPERATIVE effort to increase understanding among peoples is one of the four or five primary instruments for promoting world order and peace. Understanding does not of itself guarantee order and peace: but order and peace, with preservation of democratic ways of living, cannot be achieved without understanding.

International intercourse no longer lies wholly within the province of Foreign Offices; nor are decisions affecting the welfare of nations definitively made for them by heads of state. Foreign policy is becoming increasingly the personal concern of the humblest citizen. Even now, the decisions of San Francisco, Moscow, and London are being modified and reshaped in the committee rooms of Congress and the town halls of New Hampshire, the salons of Passy and the *bistros* of Normandy, the pubs of Whitechapel and the clubrooms of Westminster. The hurried midnight audiences of envoys bearing coded ultimatums are giving way to open conferences, whose delegates include not only diplomats but also chosen representatives of business, professional, and labor groups who speak for articulate thousands.

Over these conferences, which for many years to come will attempt to shape world co-operation, there must preside an atmosphere of genuine mutual trust and respect if there is to be any enduring success. Men must approach their differences in a climate not subject to sudden electrical storms. Such a climate can be created only by the tolerant sympathy that springs from reasoned understanding of the historic customs, values, and aspirations of all peoples. Man does not come to respect his neighbor through fiat or pious resolve. Understanding connotes knowing. Knowing connotes learning.

But it is not enough that delegates to international conferences be mentally prepared for their work. In essence, they are but the spokesmen of the people. Learning, knowing, and understanding must reach beyond the few to the many, lest the many, through ignorance, undo the labors of the few.

On what, then, must the people feed in order to be capable of reaching wise decisions? Not on propaganda, surely; fortunately, an overdose of spoon-fed words and images has immunized the world against its most obvious forms at least. The surest antidote for ignorance and deceit is the widest possible exchange of objectively realistic information—*true* information, not merely *more* information; *true* information, not merely, as those who would have us simply write the First Amendment into international law seem to suggest, the *unhindered flow* of information! There is evidence that a mere quantitative increase in the flow of words and images across national borders may replace ignorance with prejudice and distortion rather than with understanding.

For thirty years, United States press associations have waged an intensive campaign to increase the flow of words and pictures between this country and its Latin-American neighbors. In the opinion of Professor Hernane Tavares do Sa of the University of Sao Paulo, the chief result has been to etch more deeply in North American minds the concept of Latin "picturesqueness" and other "romantic nonsense," and to confirm our friends below the Rio Grande in their view of *Norte Americanos* as "culturally barren" boors.

"Mutual ignorance," Professor Tavares do Sa writes (in the *Mexican-American Review,* July, 1944), "is the great barrier that has stood between us. The press of the twenty-one republics has an essential part to play in the tearing down of this barrier. So far, both the press of the United States and that of Latin America have failed dismally."

It is perhaps significant that those peoples which through the years have enjoyed widest access to the means of international communication often have retained more distorted images of others than peoples living in relative ignorance of the outer world. Among the many examples of misunderstanding about America that have come to light during the war, the most incredible have involved, not Borneo bushmen, but western Europeans who had seen dozens of Hollywood movies.

The problem, then, is twofold. It is that of bringing the physical facilities for transmitting words and images across national boundaries within the reach of all; of lowering and, wherever possible, removing the barriers erected at those boundaries. It is also that of achieving a degree of quality, accuracy, and total balance calculated to give a fair picture of the life of each country to all the world. And we cannot assume that achievement of the first automatically will produce the second.

UNFINISHED BUSINESS

Before the war the physical facilities for transmitting words and images[1] across national boundaries were altogether inadequate for the task of carrying true information to all peoples. Four-fifths of the earth's surface did not have access to direct, twenty-four-hour telecommunication services. Except for a score of the world's principal cities, existing cable, radiotelegraph, and radiotelephone networks could not carry, in addition to the commercial traffic which was their primary concern, a volume of informational material sufficient to give a balanced and accurate picture of any people. Even where facilities were available, the tolls charged had the effect of discouraging adequate volume. Obsolescent cables, charging the highest tolls for limited wordage, could not cope with the newer forms of telecommunications, such as facsimile. Similarly, nine-tenths of the earth's peoples were denied adequate air-mail and air-express services.

Today, thanks to technological facilities accelerated by war uses, adequate telecommunication and air facilities exist. But the bulk of war-built facilities are the properties of the military

[1] By "words" and "images" we mean books, magazines, newspapers, mats, plastic plates, photographic prints and negatives, filmstrips, newsreels, motion pictures, voice radio broadcasts, dot-dash press files, radiophoto, and facsimile.

branches of governments. Many of the networks depend on terminal facilities in foreign territory granted only for the period of hostilities. Some terminal and relay facilities were never realized even on a wartime basis. Tolls on private networks remain beyond the reach of poorer editors and radio-station managers. The question of whether postwar telecommunication and air facilities[2] will be adequate for the task of disseminating true information to all the world therefore remains for the moment unanswered.

The barriers in the way of communication of words and images across national boundaries are formidable—barriers of language, of religion, of social custom, of literacy, and of governmental restrictions at national borders. They make of international mass communication something more than domestic communication writ large.

Of the more than a billion adults in the world, only about one out of four can read more than a few words or characters in his own tongue. During the war, when we and others used short-wave voice broadcasts to tell our story from day to day to all in other lands who would listen, we had to employ forty to forty-five different languages and dialects to reach them. Even where words are intelligible as words, they do not always convey the same meanings. Some words and pictures, quite harmless in the country of origin, give offense elsewhere because of different religious or social customs. "To make love" does not mean "to pay court" to a Frenchman; it does not convey any meaning to a Melanesian. Movie embraces embarrass Chinese, who do not kiss in public. A newsreel shot of an Argentine beef barbecue will empty a theater of Hindus.

Then there are the legal-administrative barriers erected at national frontiers. It is hard to get foreign news in. Many countries do not permit foreign news agencies to sell their products directly to any of their interested publications but insist on foreigners

[2] It is our assumption that transport of printed matter, mats, prints, and films by fast air mail and air express will be provided for adequately in the plans going forward for postwar international transport of air mail under the general regulations of the International Postal Union. We have not, therefore, included in our recommendations any proposals relative to such service.

dealing with "official" domestic agencies, which often distort and, still more often, suppress items thus handled. Some countries, by "persuasion" rather than by statute, prohibit the importation of certain types of news altogether. And, finally, foreign news sometimes is denied passage across national frontiers through denial of access at fair rates to communications facilities.

Getting news out of a country often is even more difficult. For years correspondents have complained of denial of equal and unhampered access to news sources—particularly official government sources. Censorship is another bugbear—not only the open deletion or suppression of dispatches but the many more subtle forms of indirect censorship: secret deletion or suppression, arbitrary delays in transmission, threat of expulsion or physical violence, loss of working permits and other privileges, or, in reverse, the offering of bribes.

Foreign newspapers and magazines are barred from sale in some countries. Periodicals which succeed in leaping this hurdle are subject to the seizure of entire editions at the whim of authorities. Motion-picture exporters groan under fifty-eight separate restrictions, ranging all the way from arbitrary quotas of two or more homemade films for every import, to graduated fees for the dubbing-in of subtitles in the language of the country. The flow of books across national frontiers is hampered by copyright confusion arising, in part, from the refusal of the United States to adhere to any general international copyright convention.

It is not clear whether in peacetime any nation will attempt to perpetuate the wartime devices designed to prevent listening to international short-wave voice broadcasts. Even in wartime the barriers erected were not too successful. They ranged from legal prohibitions against listening to foreign broadcasts, removing short-wave reception gadgets from all home receivers, conscious interference with enemy programs by broadcasting noise effects on the same frequencies (jamming), to a confiscation of all private receiving sets and limiting radio reception to receivers in public places or by telephone controlled from a central source. All but the last of these devices were only partially effective in shutting out foreign news by short wave, and it is not likely to be continued in time of peace. No attempts of a modern King Canute to sweep back the short waves from his country's national shoreline is likely to prevail. Voice broadcasting across national borders remains the instrument of international communication least subject to man-made barriers.

THE NEED IS NOW

Not so obvious, but most significant of all, there is the greater dependence of peoples separated by great distances and political boundaries upon the mass-communication media for knowledge and understanding of the activities, customs, purposes, and attitudes of other peoples.

This is a difference of degree, but a major difference nonetheless. In municipal affairs a newspaper may distort the facts and paint a false picture of a local group or issue. But it is only one source of community knowledge. There is firsthand observation and personal contact and talk in the neighborhood, club, lodge, and church to check it.

On a state and national scale, the alternative, informal sources of information are fewer. But most citizens of the United States are equipped with at least eight years of formal schooling that includes some history, civics, sociology, and current events. And Americans and Britons at least do get around (in a peacetime, tire-and-gas-supplied world); we talk directly with the people who have been places and seen things.

Moreover, aside from the general press, radio, and newsreels, there are specialized publications, including serious magazines and books in profusion, as well as lectures, round tables, and discussion groups. Thus, although in domestic affairs in the United States, the British Commonwealth, and elsewhere the mass circulation media have a power over the minds and attitudes of the citizenry, it is a power with very real limitations. Its persuasions must be substantially congruent with the facts and experiences otherwise available.

In the field of foreign information, the alternative checks are much less adequate. There are foreign travelers, to be sure, but they are a tiny fragment of the population. Undoubtedly we shall, with the aid of postwar aviation, increase the flow of international observers. Paradoxically, returned soldiers and displaced persons, far from contributing a wholesome balance to understanding among peoples, are likely, because of their atypical experiences, to increase the ratio of superficial judgments which impede rather than facilitate understanding.

But to a great extent the knowledge of specific events, the understanding of the people as a whole in Russia, China, New Guinea, and Brazil possessed by the people of Kansas will be that gained from press dispatches, radio broadcasts, movies, magazines, and books; and so also, and in even greater degree, will be the knowledge of the life and people in Kansas held by citizens in other lands.

The importance of this fact in the continuing struggle to establish a stable, peaceful world society can hardly be overemphasized. What it means in simplest terms is that the directors of mass-communication media everywhere must come to regard themselves as being no less responsible for the shape of the world than Foreign Offices and parliaments.

Because, then, of the primary importance of promoting international understanding and because of the primary importance of mass-communication media in the performance of this function, we must examine thoroughly the adequacy and potentialities of the existing instruments of international mass communication and, where they are inadequate, provide additional instruments for the task. In short, we must apply to this particular field the same tests we are applying to the whole broad field of international relations.

Nor can we afford to linger over the solution. There is a special urgency about the problem of international communication; and there are special circumstances which will determine the form and extent of freedom of the press in foreign lands. Large parts of Europe and Asia have been liberated from the domination of regimes which consciously aimed at denial of free exchange of information and erected impressive machinery for manipulating words and other symbols to serve a special set of governmental purposes. Liberation, in turn, involves a destruction of public order and the usual machinery of economic activity. Thus a major concern over large areas is that of personal security and authority among peoples deprived for years (in some cases for more than a decade) of free exchange of information.

Freedom of the press is peculiarly the child of confidence, security, and stability. It almost never lives undiminished in times of war, disorder, and revolution. This circumstance must be clearly recognized in any practical plans for extending the limits of free expression of criticism in the war-ravaged lands.

Nowhere has this important fact been more graphically illustrated than in liberated Italy. When, early in 1944, the Allied Control Commission first laid plans to turn back to Italian private industry the dissemination of domestic and world news, it became evident that the move would have to be delayed until a handful of Italians who had never been tainted with Fascist journalism could be gathered from four corners of the globe and trained for the task of organizing a co-operative press association and launching a half-dozen newspapers. Not until a year later was the transfer formally effected—and even yet the results are in doubt. Not only had Italian editors lost their contacts with the sources of truth; the Italian people had temporarily lost some of their capacity to differentiate between truth and untruth. This problem, in even more acute form, is being encountered in Germany and Japan.

In the second place, the four major partners of the United States in shaping the postwar machinery and practice of international intercourse are Russia, which has firmly held ideas and established practices in relation to the free exchange of information in contrast to our own; China, with a practice if not theory much more like Russia's than ours; France, with a long pre-war record of press venality; and Great Britain, a direct competitor in the task of furnishing words and images to the English-speaking world, with whom we must work out some basis for co-operation if this otherwise healthy competition is not to end in bitter rivalries and animosities.

That these five powers must secure the widest possible basis for common agreement in the field of international communication goes without saying. That this enormous task will require the highest type of tolerant statesmanship, on the part not only of our diplomats but of the owners of the mass-communication media themselves, is equally clear. It may be that, given this tolerance—and a tolerance among the readers themselves, lest sudden access to facts breed cynicism—time and growing confidence will narrow the breach. Not only must the effort be made; it must be made at once, and it must be sustained for as long as may be required. Failure would lead inevitably to a rapid acceleration of the already noted sealing-off of peoples from peoples, the substitution of slanted propaganda for truth within these walled "zones of influence," and ultimately the reappearance of those nationalistic neuroses that plunge their victims into war, a catastrophe that now clearly would mean the suicide of civilization.

Finally, whatever the official views of their governments, more people than ever in modern history are genuinely eager to understand each other and as genuinely eager to get hold of the materials with which this can be accomplished. There is a hungering for truth. In part this may be merely a reaction to the long blackout of reliable information. To some extent it may reflect the artificial stimulation of attractive free information supplied to people in out-of-the-way places by the governments of the United States, Great Britain, and their allies. If this hunger is not fed, if it is not fed properly, if there is a lag between wartime developments and peace machinery for the supply of information, the hunger is likely to diminish, and with it the capacity to assimilate true information.

THE TIME IS NOW

The special urgency for an increase in exchange of information across national boundaries is matched by equally special and new opportunities to create a network of communication which can reach the whole habitable globe with a rich variety of words and pictures designed to spread knowledge and understanding of cultures heretofore obscured by ignorance, distance, and suspicion.

This opportunity is created by major technological improvements in rapid, cheap, long-distance communication of words and images.

Among these may be listed amazing advances in wireless transmission, including speeds of eight hundred words a minute; the perfecting of sending and receiving apparatus which renders pirating impracticable; the near-elimination of interruptions due to adverse atmospheric conditions; and the development of four-color facsimile, which makes it possible to transmit photographs and whole pages of books and periodicals in any desired language.

The effect of these and other improvements, many of them greatly accelerated by rapid and extensive wartime utilization, is to throw open the whole habitable earth to daily, hourly, news reports, costing a fraction of a cent a word to disseminate, and to a hitherto undreamed-of diet of news, discussion, music, and entertainment by voice radio, free to the listener.

More familiar, but perhaps not yet appreciated in its full significance for the exchange of information, is the use of air-mail and air-express service for the world-wide distribution of film-strips, newsreels, feature motion pictures, and plates and mats for newspapers, magazines, and books. Within a matter of years, perhaps months, it will be possible for a film or periodical originating at one point to be distributed and exhibited throughout the globe in two or three days. Whole pages of magazines can now be taken off on cellophane mats, light as feathers, and flown to printing plants over the world, thus making possible the simultaneous publication on five continents of a complete magazine forty-eight hours after the material has been written in a central editorial office in New York, London, Paris, Moscow, or Chungking.

Less spectacular is the emergence of processes for cheap printing of books and magazines in large quantity, so that their cost brings them within the range of vastly larger and more diffused customer groups. It is now physically possible to make the most informative literature of all countries available to all who want to be informed, at less than the equivalent of 25 cents a copy.

The war has given us a preview of how these technological improvements can be used. The United States Army and Navy have developed telecommunications networks reaching the remotest parts of five continents and the seven seas from compact nerve centers in Washington. The British War Office and Admiralty, although somewhat more dependent on pre-war and in some instances obsolescent facilities, have expanded them to reach still other areas. Russia, starting from scratch, has tightened the link between Europe and the China Sea. It is estimated that the combined facilities of the Allies reached seven times as many points as were reached before the war, with eighteen times the pre-war volume, and at greatly accelerated speed. In the transmission of radiophotos alone, the number of points regularly serviced from New York, London, and Moscow has increased sixty fold.

The story of the war-developed air networks of the Allies is even more dramatic, and at the same time better known. It is sufficient to say here that if the United States Army's Air Transport Command had carried on its peak wartime routes newspapers, magazines, books, radio recordings, and film, instead of troops and weapons, 40 per cent of the globe would have been no more than seventy-two hours behind New York in mail deliveries.

The 1930's witnessed a spectacular development of short-wave voice broadcasting. Before the war, Russia, Germany, Italy, Great Britain, France, and the Netherlands had begun to build up programs designed to reach their imperial possessions, their nationals in other lands, and their immediate neighbors, in whom they had a special propaganda interest. With the war, all the combatants and practically all the neutrals developed broadcasts in scores of languages sent out by powerful transmitters halfway around the globe. With the war's end, this network of more than three hundred and sixty transmitters in more than fifty national states, sending around the world more than two thousand words a minute in forty-odd languages and manned by thousands of skilled linguists and scriptwriters, became available for the more constructive purposes of peace.

As part of our own war effort, the Overseas Branch of the Office of War Information (O.W.I.) and the Office of Inter-American Affairs (O.I.A.A.) used all the newer devices to direct press dispatches, feature stories, pictures, maps, cartoons, books, magazines, films, posters, exhibits, and voice broadcasts about America and her friends at an estimated billion[3] persons, 95 per cent of whom never before had had access to any such material. The British Ministry of Information (M.O.I.) projected the Commonwealth with an even larger volume of material; and Globe Reuter, a private British press association working closely with M.O.I., has literally saturated the globe with up-to-the-minute world news around the clock. Russia has not neglected the information field; and already liberated France is offering broadcast news on a global basis.

It has become a truism that the scientists who unlocked the secret of atomic power confronted our society with a choice between integration and disintegration. Fortunately for us all, science has also given us a timely clue to the secret of survival. Modern airplanes and wireless transmission of facsimile have made of literature published anywhere in the world a potential instrument of global understanding. International voice broadcasting and television have made it possible for the remotest areas to share in the actual writing of history. The very oceans have become the "back fences" of a world community in which all men are neighbors. What is now urgently required is to insure that these new tools are used boldly and constructively to link mankind harmoniously.

[3] This figure is an O.W.I.–O.I.A.A. readership-listenership estimate based on the evidence of newspaper and magazine clippings, radio monitoring reports, and attendance checks.

2

THE OBJECTIVE

WHAT is needed in the field of international communication is simple enough to state. It is the linking of all the habitable parts of the globe with abundant, cheap, significant, true information about the world from day to day, so that all men increasingly may have the opportunity to learn, know, and understand each other.

The Commission on the Freedom of the Press declares, in its statement (pp. v, vi, vii above) that the action necessary to attain this objective would include (1) the improvement of physical facilities and operating mechanisms so as to bring about the communication of words and images across national borders as abundantly, as cheaply, as quickly, as efficiently, and over as wide an area as possible; (2) the progressive removal of political barriers and the lessening of economic restrictions which impede the free flow of information across national borders; and (3) the improvement of the accuracy, representative character, and quality of the words and images transmitted in international communication.

This is obviously a program to be shared by many agencies and many persons in many lands. In those countries in which private companies have shown a capacity for serving the public interest and where, in consequence, they are permitted to operate without unwarranted interference by their governments, the opportunities which lie before them are very great. Thus in our own country, in the British Commonwealth, in Norway, Sweden, Denmark, Switzerland, France, Belgium, and the Netherlands, in some parts of Latin America, and perhaps one day in Germany, Italy, and those other countries which still lie under the uncertain cloud of postwar reconstruction, commercial agencies will share the major responsibility, as well as the major opportunity, for improving understanding among peoples.

But they must look beyond short-term advantage and immediate profit if they are to perform their tasks promptly and adequately. They must recognize frankly that the need to know runs almost in inverse ratio to the ability to pay, and they must devise means of reaching those who can pay little or nothing. They must realize that the most readily marketable words and images may not necessarily be the most truthful and that the responsibility to tell the truth includes the obligation to tell the *whole* story, even though parts of the story must be published without profit.

In practice, this is likely to involve nothing more revolutionary than the adaptation of means which the press and other media themselves long since have employed. Thus the principle of charges graduated according to ability to pay has been used by the American motion-picture industry to reach thousands of crude fifty- or one hundred-seat theaters in out-of-the-way places of the world with a product costing millions per unit to produce; it has been used by all commercial press associations and feature syndicates to bring to the smallest towns in America world news coverage more complete than that available in most European capitals; it has been used by numerous book-publishers here and abroad to place living literature in the hands of tens of millions instead of tens of thousands. And it is to be remarked that in none of these instances did the experiment prove unprofitable in the long run.

The principle of co-operative, nonprofit service is the basis of the Associated Press and several similar agencies, like the Swedish Tidningarnas Telegrambyraa, and of the press radiotelegraph carrier, Press Wireless, Incorporated.

Examples of the application of the principle of government-industry co-operation are even more numerous. On the nonsubsidy level, every commercial attaché in a diplomatic mission is such a symbol. On the subsidy level, government-industry co-operation is responsible for nine-tenths of the existing telecommunications facilities throughout the world. It was an indispensable ingredient in the development of the air lines. The second-class mailing privilege constitutes an outright subsidy to the press. Even the corporate income tax laws were written in such a way that the highest-priced war correspondent represented for the publisher or radio network executive an annual out-of-pocket expenditure of only a few hundred dollars.

Government-industry co-operation may be developed by the formation of nonprofit foundations, societies, and corporations, or by the greater utilization of existing foundations, societies, and corporations, to stimulate understanding among peoples through the setting-up of libraries and other information centers; the encouragement of a wider dissemination of literature, pictures, and films; and the promotion of cultural and informational exchanges of all types. Indeed, the authors regard as remarkable the fact that the initiative for some device on the order and scale of the wartime Advertising Council has not yet come, either from the mass-communications media in this country or from those corporations not directly concerned with the interchange of words and images but nonetheless dependent for the success of their own international undertakings upon the good opinion of America abroad.

Yet, although we urge that, wherever possible, governments encourage private companies to shoulder the major burden of improving understanding among peoples, we must not lose sight of the fact that they will not be able to do the whole job. That this is indisputably so is evidenced by the fact that long before the war our own government, which did far less in the informational field than any other major nation, was an affirmative contributor to the stimulation of understanding among peoples. Its numerous pamphlets and other literature, its program of book translations for schools, it work in nontheatrical documentary films, its occasional broadcasts, the related work of the Office of Education and similar bureaus, the State Department's daily *News Bulletin* and servicing of texts of government documents for the use of press-association representatives abroad as well as for members of the diplomatic missions—these and many similar activities have been carried on for years, with the knowledge and approval of private companies not interested in performing such valuable, yet commercially unprofitable, tasks.

The necessity of government participation in the informational field has been further underlined by the war. Nineteen-twentieths of the globe did not have easy access to truthful, abundant world news until the United States and British governments, compelled by military and political considerations to fill the vacuum, began to supply it. During this three- to six-year emergency period, M.O.I., O.W.I., and O.I.A.A. increased the world's awareness of British and American books and magazines one hundred fold. Faithful picturization of peoples and events in motion pictures is peculiarly associated with the entry of government agencies into the field. Similarly, government operation of short-wave broadcasts from America swelled the volume from a few experimental hours daily to round-the-clock operations to be compared with those of the domestic radio networks.

Clearly, the task of stimulating understanding among peoples through the mass-comunication media is one that must be shared by governments and private agencies. It must not be vitiated by baseless rivalries between the two or by lack of co-ordination. For these reasons there is need, in this and in other countries, of bringing into relation to each other the hundreds of corporations, individuals, government agencies, associations, societies, and foundations engaged in exchange of information across national boundaries, so that existing facilities and energies will be fully used, so that gaps will be filled, and so that new instruments and facilities can be created where there is shown to be a need for them.

At the international level, modest beginnings have been made in the form of committees, commissions, and bureaus to co-ordinate national physical facilities and promote fragmentary cultural exchange. These need to be boldly and vigorously developed under the United Nations Organization in the years ahead. This report is an attempt to sketch the general pattern for both the national and the international structure in line with these objectives.

3

THE PHYSICAL INSTRUMENTS

WHAT are the present instruments and processes in international communication? What is their origin, history, and present functioning? How adequate are they for the tasks ahead? What are the proposals for change in operations calculated to achieve our objectives?

THE TELECOMMUNICATION SERVICES

In contrast to the United States, the governments of virtually all countries are directly involved in the business of furnishing telecommunications[1] services. Almost all own and operate their

[1] "Telecommunications" as used in this report is an inclusive term. As officially defined by international convention it includes "any telegraph or telephone communication of signs, signals, writings, images, and sounds of any nature, by wire, radio [wireless], or other systems or processes of electric or visual (semaphore) signalling." The impulse may be sent by clicking a key in long and short intervals to produce dot-dash (international Morse code symbols) audible to the human ear. Through the use of vacuum tubes, the impulses may reproduce other sounds, such as the human voice and music. The impulse may operate typing machines at the receiving end or perforate tape capable of operating typing machines. Or by the use of photoelectric "scanning" devices the impulse may produce photographic images at the receiving end, including whole pages of printed matter, written script in languages the operator does not comprehend, diagrams, still or motion pictures.

Theoretically, both cables (for the purposes of our report everything transmitted by wire, whether submarine cable or land line, will be referred to as "cables") and wireless can provide all these forms of service. Actually, some of the submarine cables linking the United States with the other parts of the world are of such ancient design that they can carry only dot-dash, and that at speeds averaging 40–60 words a minute, although the most modern cables can carry pictures and operate at greater speeds, some carrying as many as 200 words a minute.

Originally, telecommunication was from one point to another specific point. For obvious reasons, cables cannot reach more than a certain number of fixed termini in a single operation. Wireless, on the other hand, can be so designed

domestic telegraph systems exclusively and, with the exception of Latin America, where foreign operators have moved in, the telephones as well. As to external facilities, the ratio of government interest varies: Japan, Norway, and Switzerland own and operate all telecommunications; the governments of Belgium, Sweden, and Finland own some cables and all wireless facilities; the British government recently announced its intention to nationalize all cable

---

as to transmit from one point to another, or, through what we now know as "broadcasting," it can be addressed from a single point to an unlimited number of receivers within a large area. This broadcasting method has recently been developed for the use of press associations to send news in dot-dash code and facsimile simultaneously to known receivers in a large area. In voice broadcasting, the receiver is a member of the public who does not pay for the service. In commercial newscasting by dot-dash or facsimile, the receiver pays for the service.

We can then divide the various types of telecommunication into the following: (*a*) point-to-point cable (and land-line telegraph); (*b*) point-to-point radio (wireless) telegraph; (*c*) point-to-point radio (wireless) telephone; (*d*) voice and music radio (wireless) broadcasting; (*e*) multiple-address radio (wireless) newscasting, usually by dot-dash (also called "multiple-destination newscasting").

This classification conceals further flexibility. All but the first facility (i.e., cable) can be used technically to transmit dot-dash, voice and teletypewriter impulses, and complete images, such as pictures and pages of type and script. Legally, however, there are limitations by international convention on such interchangeable use of channels. The international voice-broadcast frequencies under present international assignment of channels may not be used for multiple address. Similarly, the United States companies licensed to engage in multiple-address newscasting are not permitted by international convention to broadcast voice or music programs over the frequencies assigned for multiple address (although they may carry them from one point to another for rebroadcast).

Finally, although all wireless transmission, whether point-to-point or broadcast, may employ short, medium, or long wave, such telecommunications to and from the United States usually involve distances of more than a thousand miles, and short wave is used. In popular terminology, international voice broadcasting has been identified with short wave, although contiguous European countries frequently use medium wave for international broadcasts. And, conversely, point-to-point international radiotelegraph, radiotelephone, and multiple-address newscasts normally use short wave.

No consideration in this report is given to television and frequency modulation, both of which are of great importance for the future in domestic mass communication. This is because both are at present limited in distance of transmission to the range of the horizon, hence are not currently involved in direct international telecommunication to and from the United States. Very short waves are being developed, however, for radio-relays paralleling wire lines. Eventually, such systems will go from the United States into Canada, Mexico, and Cuba, thus enlarging the area of international telecommunication.

and wireless facilities; in Greece, Egypt, Portugal, and most Latin-American countries neither the government nor national industry controls the telecommunications links with the outer world, enterprising foreigners (usually either the International Telephone and Telegraph Company or Cable and Wireless, Limited, with Radio Corporation of America appearing also as part of various combinations of foreign groups) having taken over such services by long-term lease.

Two nations clearly dominate the international field: Britain, with 190,000 nautical miles of cables, 63,000 miles of point-to-point wireless circuits, and a potential for broadcasting voice radio, dot-dash, and facsimile to literally every part of the globe; and the United States, with 94,000 miles of cables, 236,000 miles of point-to-point wireless telegraph, and a broadcast potential limited only by the lack of suitable permanent relay points to circumvent the Auroral Zone about the North Pole—a natural phenomenon that does not plague the more fortunately located British, over whose empire the radio signals never fade. The comparison is at once significant and misleading; it indicates that wireless is rapidly surpassing cables, which is true, and that America's predominance in the newer medium has challenged Britain's long-time leadership in international telecommunications, which also is true; but it might be taken as prima facie evidence that America's leadership itself will go unchallenged, and that depends upon what America does, not later than 1946, to consolidate its position. Our present advantage is largely a wartime phenomenon.

The United States has missed the boat on at least two previous occasions. The first was when Cyrus Field, Peter Cooper, and other wise Americans proposed a submarine cable to link America with Europe. It was not the United States government but the British, long aware of the value to a nation with global political and economic interests of rapid, reliable communications, which guaranteed the pioneers a 5 per cent profit for as long as their venture functioned. After that Britain combed the empire for investors willing to lay cables under government guaranties. When that did not work, the government laid them itself, notably the All Red

Route from London to Australia, which embraces the two longest submarine cable spans in existence. Guglielmo Marconi, suffering substantially the same fate in his homeland that Field and Cooper had encountered in theirs, found a welcome in England, where his privately owned Wireless Telegraph Company soon established a radiotelegraph network embracing most of the empire. British trade undoubtedly gained in consequence of these two moves. And during World War I the unquestioned dominance of London as the center of world communications proved of incalculable military, news, and propaganda value.

The rapid development of wireless communication by our engineers virtually thrust upon Americans a second opportunity to take the lead in global telecommunications. This, too, was lost, and for a variety of reasons. To begin with, much of the pioneering in radiotelegraphy from the United States was done by R.C.A., which was interested primarily in the development of a domestic voice radio broadcast network. The other big company in the field, I.T.&T., had invested heavily in cables and still could not believe that the newer device would ever offer anything more than a supplementary "feeder" service.

Wireless telegraph circuits, like cables, require terminal facilities. Like cables, radio to reach around the globe needs automatic relay points to "boost" the signal as it begins to fade. Both requirements, in the case of the United States, involve treaties with foreign powers, because we lack Britain's conveniently placed stepping-stones around the globe. Such treaties were not sought at the Versailles peace table. Given breathing space, the British government spun its own wireless web—a web which soon assumed the characteristics of monopoly in that it denied to rivals the right to operate circuits directly from their own countries to British Empire points. Meantime, but for the swift intervention of our Navy Department, the British in 1919 might have obtained exclusive control of the Alexanderson "alternator," a General Electric product, and the DeForest tube, which would have set American wireless (and domestic radio) development back a decade.

If the efficiency and economy of radiotelegraph did not impress cable minded Americans with the need to seize early leadership, it made a very deep impression on their British counterparts. Faced with the double threat of rate and service competition from the British Post Office and the Marconi companies and with the ever present rivalry of the American cable companies, British cable owners saw their revenues dwindling and their stocks falling off. Without hesitation, they determined to save their investments by using government aid to subdue their wireless competitors. As neither the War Office nor the Admiralty was completely sold on wireless, the government reacted promptly to their proposal, and according to expectation. An Imperial Wireless and Cable Conference was hurriedly summoned. The result was the formation, in 1929, of two "chosen instruments," one a holding and the other an operating corporation, but both known as Cable and Wireless. Into the consolidation went the private companies' 165,000 miles of cables and practically all of the government's 25,000, the point-to-point radio stations and manufacturing interests of the British Marconi company, and some of the radiotelegraph facilities of the British Post Office. The offer of shares to the public was accompanied by newspaper stories mentioning an expected 6 per cent profit.

Actually the 6 per cent was never approached, and in 1936 the government was obliged to step in again. Rentals of government facilities amounting to a quarter of a million pounds a year were canceled in exchange for government ownership of 9 per cent of the stock; dividends were cut sharply; the company's license was extended to insure greater monopoly benefits; and a uniform maximum empire rate of 1*s* 3*d*. was inaugurated for messages between any two points in the Commonwealth, as a means of meeting foreign wireless competition, chiefly from the Royal Netherlands Post Office. Two years later there was instituted a uniform press rate of a penny (then 2 cents, now 1½ cents, American) a word between any two points in the empire. Cable and Wireless seemed on the way to a secure, if somewhat limited, future, although the Dutch and the French also, despite their heavy investment in cables, were expanding the wireless links with their own far-flung empires.

Indeed, telecommunications had become one of the integral elements of colonial development.

Eighteen months after the new arrangement had been solemnized in the Imperial Telegraphs Act, Hitler attacked Poland. Official government telecommunications traffic immediately assumed such proportions as to assure Cable and Wireless of steady dividends, and at the same time to obscure temporarily the handwriting on every cable-owner's wall.

The British cable-owners had thought so little of international broadcasting that they had left the British Post Office in possession of a few transmitters for experimental multiple-address newscasting and marginal services, and the thriving B.B.C. in command of its own voice-broadcasting facilities. Before the war, B.B.C. began a vigorous program of international broadcasting of news and comment in Italian, Spanish, and Arabic, mainly to counteract Mussolini's radio broadcasting propaganda to the Arab world. To the British Ministry of Information and Reuter, the powerful world-wide press association which operated virtually as a wartime arm of M.O.I., certain elementary facts soon became apparent: (1) Cable and Wireless, Limited, never very much impressed with the need for speed in handling press dispatches, was becoming, thanks to its monopoly position and the exigencies of wartime, even more dilatory in handling press copy; (2) the broadcasting of news (newscasting) by dot-dash on what is known as the multiple-address principle would bring the unit cost very much lower than Cable and Wireless' 1-penny empire press rate; (3) medium- and short-wave voice radio broadcasts could reach places (occupied Europe, for example) with news beyond the practical reach of dot-dash.

Accordingly, M.O.I. supplied B.B.C. bountifully with news for voice broadcasts and encouraged the Post Office to build new transmitters so that Reuter could reach literally all the world with dot-dash. The results were spectacular in winning friends for a beleaguered nation and contributed powerfully to the Allied cause in occupied countries. But the fact that much of the world was seeing America's war effort through British eyes disturbed many

Americans, notably the senators who, in 1943, toured the Mediterranean and Pacific battle-fronts. Assuming that Reuter's advantage stemmed from the Cable and Wireless monopoly which Reuter virtually had ceased to use (Cable and Wireless carried only 2½ per cent of Reuter's file in 1944), these senators returned to join in the clamor for a merger of this country's competing telecommunications companies.

The American telecommunications structure during the years of its rapid development following World War I assumed a form quite different from the British and, indeed, from those of all other countries. There developed actually nine American-owned but not government-owned telecommunications companies, most of which are competing for the same business. There are five major corporations, one of which competes directly with the other four in only a small marginal field confined to the point-to-point transmission of voice radio programs for rebroadcast; and four lesser ones, none of which handles much normal commercial message traffic. the nine companies are discussed below.

I. INTERNATIONAL TELEPHONE AND TELEGRAPH CORPORATION

This giant holding company's wholly owned Commercial Cable Company operates four trans-Atlantic cables and two channels of a Western Union cable to the Azores. Together with two cables put out of commission during the war, these total 22,000 nautical miles. The capacity of the six plus the two channels leased from Western Union is 575 words a minute.

I.T.&T.'s wholly owned All America Cable and Radio, Incorporated, blankets Central America, the Caribbean, and the coasts of South America with five submarine cables, totaling 29,000 nautical miles. Their over-all capacity is 340 words a minute.

The Commercial Pacific Cable Company, of which I.T.&T. is a 25 per cent stockholder (the British Cable and Wireless controls 50 per cent; Great Northern, a Danish company, the other 25), operates the only trans-Pacific cable from the United States, which runs 10,000 nautical miles to Shanghai. The capacity of this cable's dual channels is 100 words a minute.

The corporation's wholly owned Mackay Radio and Telegraph Company operates a radiotelegraph network reaching many parts of the world over forty-two circuits, including a widely extended ship-to-shore service.

A smaller subsidiary, Radio Corporation of Porto Rico, wholly owned by I.T.&T., operates a radiotelephone circuit between several points in the West Indies, connecting through its San Juan terminus with the A.T.&T. continental system in New York.

In 1944 the gross operating revenue of these five companies exceeded $18,000,000.

Scores of manufacturing and local operating subsidiaries in twenty-eight foreign countries also give I.T.&T. an important share of the international radiotelegraph market and vital telecommunications patents, some interest in short-wave voice broadcasting, and a very lively concern over the domestic politics of half the countries in the world. Stock in the parent-corporation and its subsidiaries is widely held by foreign nationals.

II. WESTERN UNION

This company operates the other eight trans-Atlantic cables[2] controlled by the United States, leasing five of them from their British owners for ninety-nine years. In addition, it operates a cable from the United States to the Azores, connecting there with foreign-owned cables to Europe; a cable from New York to Barbados, connecting with circuits to South American points; three cables to Havana, connecting with circuits to other points in the West Indies; and the Mexican Telegraph Company cable (partly owned by Western Union, the other 40 per cent by All America Cables), linking Galveston, Texas, with the cities of Mexico.

The total Western Union cable mileage is 31,623 nautical miles. Across the Atlantic it furnishes 26 channels capable of carrying 1,170 words a minute. In 1944 the gross international business was approximately $12,000,000.

[2] Of the eighteen trans-Atlantic cables in operation before the war, Cables and Wireless still operates two; the two operated by the French Telegraph and Cable Company have been interrupted.

At the time of the merger of the two domestic telegraph companies, Western Union and Postal Telegraph Company (the latter until a short time before merger a subsidiary of I.T.&T.), by Act of Congress in 1943, the Western Union Company was ordered to divest itself of its submarine cables, portions of which were laid as long ago as 1873. This dissolution was held in abeyance during the war period and has not been accomplished as yet.

III. THE RADIO CORPORATION OF AMERICA

R.C.A. Communications, Incorporated, a subsidiary of R.C.A., operating 62 circuits to foreign and overseas points, handles most of the American share of the international radiotelegraph business. With Mackay as its only substantial rival, its Radio Marine handles the ship-to-shore radiotelegraph business. R.C.A. also has an interest in both domestic and international voice broadcasting through ownership of the National Broadcasting Company. (It formerly owned the Blue Network as well.) The corporation, in addition, owns the old Victor Talking Machine Company and affiliates and a number of plants manufacturing radio equipment. R.C.A.C. in 1944 did a gross telecommunications business of about $10,000,000.

IV. THE AMERICAN TELEPHONE AND TELEGRAPH COMPANY

This company dominates the domestic telephone systems in the United States and has an almost complete monopoly of the international wireless telephone business from and to the United States: it operates wireless circuits from New York,[3] Miami, and San Francisco to 37 foreign and overseas points, where foreign telephone systems provide direct speaking connection with 95 per cent of the telephones in the world. The only other American participants are R.C.A.C., which operates for the Mutual Telephone Company of Hawaii the Honolulu terminal of A.T.&T.'s San Francisco–Hawaii circuit; and Radio Corporation of Porto Rico, the I.T.&T. subsidiary, operating the Puerto Rico terminal and direct circuits between San Juan and several West Indies points.

[3] There is only one telephone cable operating from the United States to a foreign point (Miami to Cuba), and it is not fully used.

Foreign telephone systems operate the overseas terminals of the A.T.&T. circuits, but in many instances these foreign companies are owned or controlled by the I.T.&T.

V. PRESS WIRELESS, INCORPORATED

This company, organized in 1929 by several newspapers and authorized to carry press (including radio program transmission) traffic only, operates point-to-point radiotelegraph circuits between New York and Mexico City, Havana, Santiago (Chile), Montevideo, Rio de Janeiro, Buenos Aires, Berne, Paris, London, Moscow, Berlin, Prague, and Brussels; and between Los Angeles and Khabarvosk, Manila, Shanghai, Chungking, and Tokyo. Press Wireless also offers to the press physical facilities for multiple-address newscasting to many parts of the world, the company having pioneered, along with the British Post Office, in developing this type of service. Eschewing the more lucrative commercial-message business, Press Wireless nevertheless grossed more than $2,500,000 in 1944.

VI. THE FOUR SMALLER SYSTEMS

Each of the four smaller telecommunications companies was created to serve as a means of convenient communication for an American corporation with overseas operations. Although it is not the main reason for their existence, the communications subsidiaries take commercial messages to and from other people. The four are:

The Tropical Radio Telegraph Company, a subsidiary of the United Fruit Company, which operates fifteen radiotelegraph circuits between Boston, Miami, New Orleans, and all the countries in Central America and the Caribbean. Tropical grossed more than $230,000 in 1944.

Globe Wireless, Limited, with pre-war circuits to China, the Philippines, Cuba, and Colombia, was founded by the Robert Dollar Steamship Company to handle its extensive operations, mainly in the Pacific. It was taken over by our government during the recent war but has resumed commercial operation of its New

York to Honolulu radiotelegraph circuit via San Francisco. In 1941 it grossed about $1,750,000.

United States–Liberia Radio Corporation, owned by the Firestone Tire and Rubber Company, which operates a direct radiotelegraph circuit between Akron, Ohio, and Harbel, Liberia. It does very little commercial business. In 1944 it earned less than $15,000.

The South Porto Rico Sugar Company, with a radiotelegraph circuit from Puerto Rico to Haiti, the Dominican Republic, other West Indies points, and Venezuela, carrying a very small amount of commercial traffic (approximately $3,000 gross income in 1944).

Thus, aside from these minor and special services, the United States has five commercial overseas telecommunications companies, two (Western Union and I.T.&T.) competing in the cable field, two (R.C.A. and I.T.&T.) competing in the radiotelegraph field (with a third [Press Wireless] competing for the press radiotelegraph business), and one (A.T.&T.) occupying the international telephone field. Of the five, one (Western Union) is linked in ownership with the dominating domestic telegraph system (Western Union), another with the dominating domestic telephone system (A.T.&T.), a third (R.C.A.) with one of the four national voice-broadcasting networks, a fourth (I.T.&T.) in various ways with foreign telephone systems, and the fifth (Press Wireless) owned by three press associations, a feature syndicate, and seven of the country's leading newspapers. All but one (Western Union), directly or through subsidiaries, are leading manufacturers of telecommunications equipment. And one has a subsidiary making recording disks. Together, the five companies share with Great Britain the major international telecommunications business. They would constitute a formidable aggregation of power and influence if they chose to act in unison.

VII. THE MILITARY NETWORK

Widespread as are the combined facilities of all these companies, they pale by every test when compared with the networks built within the last five years by the United States Army and Navy. Secrecy still surrounds the details of these systems put together with taxpayer's money, but several significant facts are known.

The book value of American private cables, after depreciation, is estimated at around $40,000,000; that of American radiotelegraph and radiotelephone companies is put at approximately $15,000,000. Estimates varying from $25,000,000 to $250,000,000 have been given for the combined military facilities. In any case the figure would exceed the total value of existing private American-owned radiotelegraph and radiotelephone facilities.[4]

The total mileage of the military networks is probably two or three times as great as that of the combined American private companies; and their global coverage in terms of areas reached is many times greater.

The military networks and the private industries, working in co-operation, have developed and utilized a secret formula for "scrambling" wireless messages (both point-to-point and multiple address) in such a way that they cannot be made intelligible except by a "decoding" receiver, which means that radio now affords as much security in transmission as the cables, which can be, and during the war, it is suspected, were tapped by the enemy. They handle speeds up to 800 words a minute—a turnover which has been equaled by only one private company, Press Wireless, and which compares with average cable speeds of 40–60 words a minute. The Army and Navy networks together have accommodated as many as 50,000,000 words in a day, four times the over-all cable potential of 2,500,000 and the total private wireless potential of something like 10,000,000. Moreover, the military have done wonders in subdividing channels so as to get eight times as much work from each channel, in increasing signal

[4] A first estimate of $250,000,000 was given to the Senate Committee on Interstate Commerce by the Army Signal Corps and the Navy Bureau of Communications, later revised to $162,000,000, of which $20,000,000–$25,000,000 consisted of equipment directly usable in a civilian postwar telecommunications entity. The figure is adjusted to take account of inflated costs of wartime construction but does not allow for the relatively cheap labor supplied by enlisted personnel. Also it should be noted that a substantial part of the military networks equipment is located on foreign soil which must be vacated now that the war is over.

strength, in determining ideal locations for the necessary relay points for a global system, and in perfecting automatic high-speed sending and receiving apparatus which links the nerve centers at Washington with more than a thousand fixed and mobile points throughout the world.

CABLE-WIRELESS MERGER?

Reconsideration of American telecommunications policy and organization now that the war is over is a necessity. The modern global telecommunications network of the Army will not be needed for military purposes in time of peace and must be disposed of by early summer of 1946. Something must be done also with the short-wave broadcasting facilities built during the war and operated by O.W.I. and O.I.A.A. and with no assured future under the Department of State beyond June 30, 1946. And Western Union, under the Act of Congress in 1943, legalizing a domestic telegraph monopoly, is required to divest itself entirely of its cable ownership. Thus, as regards cable and wireless communication overseas, no general return to the *status quo ante bellum* is possible.

As early as 1935 the Federal Communications Commission (F.C.C.), which regulates the rates, service, and ownership of overseas, as well as domestic, telecommunications common carriers operating in United States territory, went on record in favor of a merger of the United States cable and wireless telegraph companies. The proposal was renewed in 1943 by the then chairman of the commission, James Lawrence Fly. In the same year the Senate Committee on Interstate Commerce initiated an investigation of the merger problem. And at the insistence of the President, the State Department appointed an interdepartmental committee with Mr. Fly as chairman to develop a comprehensive postwar program for international short-wave voice broadcasting.

I. THE VARIOUS PROPOSALS

As of February, 1946, neither Congress nor the interested administrative agencies have come to any agreement on a general plan or fundamental policy for reorganization of the overseas communications units. From individual statements made at the Senate Committee hearings and elsewhere, however, there have emerged several reorganization proposals. They may be summarized as follows:

a) A Navy plan, first announced in 1944 and described at the Wheeler (Senate) Committee hearings in April, 1945, by Secretary Forrestal and Admiral Redman. It provides for compulsory merger of all American cable, radiotelegraph, and radiotelephone companies, including Press Wireless, and provides also that the military services turn over to the merged company at a fair valuation such of their war-built telecommunications facilities as are required by the merged company and not needed for peacetime military uses. Excluded from the proposed merger are aviation and safety radio services and short-wave broadcasting facilities. The Navy plan specifies representation of four or five government departments on the company's board of directors (a minority of the board membership) to guarantee that military and other governmental needs would be protected. Regulation of rates and service by the F.C.C. would apply to the merged corporation as it now is exercised over the constituent companies.

b) An earlier proposal put forward by ex-Chairman Fly of the F.C.C. for a voluntary merger to include the facilities enumerated in the Navy plan. When Paul Porter was F.C.C. chairman, he indicated at the 1945 Senate hearings that he personally favored a merger similar to that proposed by the Navy, except that he would not provide for government representation on the board of directors of the merged company, trusting rather to F.C.C. regulation as a means of guaranteeing the maintenance of necessary governmental interests in the company's policy and operations. He did not take any definite position in relation to inclusion of press and telephone in the merged entity. No official F.C.C. plan had been announced as of February, 1946.

c) A State Department proposal, presented by Assistant Secretary

Will Clayton, suggesting the maintenance of vigorous competitive units rather than comprehensive merger as the essential basis for postwar telecommunications organization. Mr. Clayton's statement was not a matured or definite proposal but was rather a dissent from the view that the case for merger had been made conclusively. He suggested as alternatives permitting merger of cable, radiotelegraph, and radiotelephone entities separately, with maintenance of full competition among the three types. More emphatically, he felt that Press Wireless performed a specialized function for the press and that it should be exempt from any merger. He suggested also that the Army might sell its war equipment to the highest bidder and that the statute requiring Western Union to dispose of its cables might be repealed, thus approaching as nearly as possible the *status quo ante,* with no merger at all.

d) A Civil Aeronautics Administration presentation approving a merger which would exclude the radiotelephone (A.T.&T.).

e) Senator Wheeler's offhand suggestion (in no sense committing him or the Senate committee) at the April, 1945, hearings that goverment ownership and operation of international telecommunications facilities might "turn out to be the answer."

None of these proposals has dealt with the problems of direct (short-wave) international voice broadcasting. The interdepartmental committee under the aegis of the State Department came to no conclusion in this field, except that there should be some direct international voice broadcasting after the war. This minimal statement of policy was made necessary by an earlier proposal made to it by the Interdepartmental Radio Advisory Committee (I.R.A.C.) that the United States abandon short-wave broadcasting. The F.C.C., as part of its comprehensive task of parceling out the entire radio spectrum to various types of services, has recommended setting aside a total of 120 channels for short-wave voice broadcasting to be shared by the United States with other countries; but this allocation is subject to co-operative agreement by all the interested nations. This is a few more frequencies than the pre-war allocation for the purpose made by international convention. Who should conduct the American short-wave voice broadcasts has not been decided by any agency, public or private.

In the public discussion of these various proposals, many, but not all, of the major factors which should be given weight in making a sound decision concerning our foreign telecommunications have been brought to focus. Some of the more important factors from the viewpoint of the citizen's interest in cheap, rapid, universal exchange of information have barely been mentioned. It is these major factors which concern us rather than the particular form of organization emerging from the interplay of forces represented by Congress, the administrative agencies, and the private companies.

II. THE FUTURE OF THE CABLES

An underlying problem, though not often mentioned, is the future of submarine cables in international telecommunications. The fact is that the cables are rapidly becoming obsolete. In a technological field in which obsolescence is reckoned in months or a year, very little that goes back in part to the 1860's is indispensable. The future belongs to speed, and three or four good radiotelegraph circuits can carry as much traffic as all the Atlantic cables combined. The future also will give a major position to facsimile or page-by-page transmission, and only one of the eighteen Atlantic cables can carry it. Moreover, cables cannot, of course, handle multiple-address newscasts or voice broadcasts. Because of their much higher capital cost per word per second, cables just cannot compete on anything like equal terms with radiotelegraph. They might now be going out of use except for the fact that telecommunications rates have been fixed by governmental authority up to the present and have been artificially maintained at levels high enough to yield a return for the cable companies above costs of operation. In this way cables now serve as a handicap to the development of cheap, universal service—a handicap which should be eliminated in any sound postwar program.

It was this handicap which the British imposed upon themselves when the cable company shareholders persuaded their government to effectuate the creation of Cable and Wireless, Limited. During the 1935–38 debates in Parliament, a British government spokesman frankly declared that the motive behind the merger was a feeling that it was "immoral" in a democracy to condemn property widely held by the citizens just because it had become obsolete. The present Cable and Wireless is not the final British solution to the problem, although present plans, so far announced, look to a system of government ownership in Britain and the separate Dominions which will retain cables as an essential part of the structure.

The two arguments given for preserving the cables in our postwar structure are on other than economic grounds: first, that they serve as a reliable stand-by means of communication when atmospheric conditions black out wireless transmissions for short periods and, second, that cables have a security feature of especial value for military and diplomatic messages. The stand-by feature was relevant when a wireless-telegraph company was limited to one route across the North Atlantic, let us say, where atmospheric blackouts occur regularly. But with a wireless network reaching around the globe under one control, alternative wireless routes can be used during blackouts in such a way that the wireless network has its own stand-by arrangements. On the other side, cable breaks, when they occur, take weeks or months, with expensive equipment, to repair. Interruption of traffic, in the meantime, is complete. As for secrecy of messages, the Army's perfection of "scrambled" transmission and reception, together with the well-founded suspicion that electronic devices enable vessels to tap cables in mid-ocean, reduce the security advantage which cables have possessed in the past.

No one suggests that the present United States cables be detached at the ends and allowed to rust peacefully in the ocean's bed, along with other of war's maritime casualties. Aside from capital costs and costs of major repairs, cables are as economical in day-to-day operation as many wireless circuits. The sensible program is to recognize frankly the increasing obsolescence of the

American cable circuits, to use them regularly and fully as part of a general communications system as long as the expenses of replacement and major repairs do not appear formidable, but to make definite financial provision for their complete amortization at an early period.

Just as important is it to be assured that neither in management nor in rate determination should any merged system be geared to cable operations. Rates should be fixed at figures sufficient only for the merged entity to make a fair return on its whole investment. As for management, any concern of which the Army war-built network is a part will be mainly a radiotelegraph company, because of the preponderance of the Army network in the total enterprise.

The problem is not, however, quite so simple as that. Whereas the volume of messages carried by wireless in any merged company would be much greater than that carried by cable, the cable companies' stock ownership, because of the great capital cost of cables, would be very large in proportion to wireless. The artificial maintenance of the cable interest in any merger must be guarded against. This could best be done by a statutory-administrative valuation formula enunciated as part of the merger authorization which would scale down the cable capital values to something nearer their present worth as computed by capitalized earnings in free competition with wireless. Another possibility is use of the device of government purchase of stock of the constituent companies and sale of stock of the merged company, the government in the transaction absorbing in an undervaluation of its own contributed equipment the uneconomic cable values. A third alternative would be to leave the cable capital values at something like their present figures in the merger but to provide in the merger statute for rapid amortization of cable capital out of earnings of the merged enterprise.

The obsolescence of cables must be paid for by someone. In the first case it would be paid for by the stockholders. (Actually, there is every reason to believe that earnings over the years have amortized the capital costs.) In the second case the taxpayers would foot the bill. In the third case those who pay telecommunications tolls would provide the liquidation funds. This problem of procedure, involving directly the competing pecuniary interests of groups in our population, is peculiarly one for congressional decision rather than for scientific determination. And if the usual method of conciliation is followed, the cost may be be shared by all three groups. But as to the necessity, in any plan, of writing off the cable capital values definitely and rapidly, there should be no compromise.

Any of the plans of merger would be equally good so far as the matter of cables is concerned. At first glance Assistant Secretary Clayton's suggestion of competition between merged cable, wireless telegraph, and wireless telephone is attractive. With such a setup in a free market without regulation, the cables would be liquidated in short order, and the problem would be solved by the operation of the rules of the game. The trouble is that telecommunications rates are not fixed by supply and demand but rather by a government regulatory commission. And whereas under the operations of a free market the investor takes his chances, under government regulation up to date he is protected against rates fixed at a point where the result would be confiscatory.[5] The Clayton suggestion might, therefore, effectively prevent the lowering of telecommunications rates and consequent extension of the service. A merger of cable and commercial radiotelegraph companies, at the least, is indicated as the means of effective modernization and lowering of rates.

III. THE DEVELOPMENT OF MULTIPLE ADDRESS

Perhaps more important than proper disposition of cables in our postwar telecommunications system is the full development of physical facilities for multiple-address press transmission to reach all habitable points on the globe. Only recently has this special kind of service been given any attention in merger proposals. From

[5] In defense of this regulatory policy it should be said that until recently experts in military and other circles felt that cables should be preserved on account of their greater security and freedom from interruption.

the viewpoint of those interested in a full and widespread exchange of information across national borders, it is a consideration of prime importance.

There is every indication that, for all except densely settled and economically advanced areas, news distribution by multiple address is the technique of the future. Judged from the viewpoint of its operating efficiency and economy, its advantages are undeniable. By adopting the broadcasting device for Morse code or facsimile transmission, with automatic reception, it means that from a single press-association source a set of news items is sent on a wide beam to an area of several thousand square miles, where it is picked up simultaneously by scores or even hundreds of contracting newspapers on radioprinter machines in individual newspaper offices. The costs of transmission are shared by all who receive the file rather than borne by individual newspapers as separate costs of cable or point-to-point radiotelegraph, plus domestic telegraph charges.

As a commercial operation, multiple-address newscasting changes the traditional habits and practices of press associations. It provides identical news service for competitors in a large area, thus upsetting the principle of "exclusive franchise" on which American press services have developed. It involves problems of pirating which will only gradually be solved in many places. It leads to complicated bookkeeping. It is not so immediately profitable as point-to-point traffic in volume between densely settled population centers, although in the long run, after a developmental period, Reuter's experience shows that it will yield profits which justify multiple-address newscasts as a commercial operation.

Its tremendous advantages in increasing the flow of information between peoples by overcoming barriers of distance and high cost mean that it should be thoroughly developed as part of our postwar communications. Actually, Press Wireless was a pioneer in the technical development of multiple-address newscasting. But it has not been developed as an operating reality to any great extent because of tardiness on the part of American press associations in urging its use and obtaining for it governmental allotment of a fair share of the all-too-scarce short-wave frequencies. As in other inventions in the communications field, Great Britain has been a pioneer in utilization. As was noted above, the British Post Office in 1939 instituted multiple address at Rugby, and since that time Reuter has used the service to cover large areas hitherto untouched by commercial press agencies. Here the promotional period is being financed by a government agency with other than commercial incentives.

Our own governmental war agencies, O.W.I. and O.I.A.A., have similarly made extensive use of multiple-address newscasts to reach directly large areas of the world which hitherto had received news from and about the United States in very small amount and only as interpreted by foreign agencies in transit from our shores. During the war period Russia also extended this type of press service to many countries. During the latter part of the war, United Press (U.P.), International News Service (I.N.S.), and Associated Press (A.P.), the last a relatively new entry in selling American news abroad directly to newspapers, began to call on Press Wireless for multiple-address facilities. Because of scarcity of available frequencies due to their wartime use by our military and government information agencies, Press Wireless was not able to build up anything equivalent to the British Rugby coverage. As a result, we find A.P. and U.P. still turning to the British government transmitters for such time on the air as is available after Reuter's extensive program is provided for.

This is obviously not a satisfactory situation. We can be assured that now, at the war's end, the editor of the obscure and relatively impecunious newspaper in the Balkans, Syria, or Thailand will have the day's news coming to him direct by teleprinter from Britain, from Russia, and probably from other major countries. O.W.I. experience indicates clearly that he wants to receive the American version of events as well. In many cases, indeed, he has come to believe, on the basis of experience, that the American agencies come nearer to what is called "objectivity" than any other. He is entitled to get our version, and it is greatly to our interest that he should get it.

Several steps are necessary. In the reallocation of radio frequencies, the F.C.C. should give *primary* consideration to applications for multiple-address newscasting channels. Fully as important is the provision of at least two powerful automatic relay points, one in the western European longitude and another in the Philippines longitude. With these, radio engineers (fortified by actual O.W.I. war experience) assure us that outgoing United States multiple-address newscasts (and also voice broadcasts) can cover the habitable globe with adequate signal strength. The Philippines relay point is probably not difficult to obtain from a diplomatic viewpoint. The European longitude relay station may be located in the International Zone of Tangier, North Africa, where the War Department already operates a transmitter. Negotiations for long-term leases or outright purchase of the small property sites (1,500–2,000 acres) needed should be pushed to completion without delay.

What form of physical facilities is best suited to operate multiple-address transmissions for the press associations? In Britain and Russia the facilities have been developed as government enterprises without giving major consideration to financial return. Although Press Wireless has been the agency to initiate multiple-address newscasting facilities, it is a fair question whether Press Wireless can pioneer a comprehensive global coverage in this field equal to that of other countries. A new and promising entry into this field may appear soon as a result of the application of the Mackay Radio and Telegraph Company (subsidiary of I.T.&T.) filed with the F.C.C. for a third-of-a-cent-a-word tariff in connection with a world-wide transmission of American news by multiple address. What is required is a system of promotion rates designed to reach all habitable areas rather than a policy of skimming the cream off the most profitable traffic. If the press associations would adopt the principle of charges employed in the United States, by which charge or service is equated with the circulation size of the newspaper, so that the metropolitan dailies pay much more for the press-association news file than the village daily, it would enable newspapers everywhere to subscribe. In their domestic services, however, the press associations have an operational reason for extending their subscribers as widely as possible. The A.P. contract with newspapers is a two-way arrangement: the member-papers furnish news to the association as well as receive news from it. And wide extent of coverage is also an important basis of U.P. and I.N.S. strength, although both these agencies obtain news from subscriber papers on a somewhat more informal basis. The same two-way process does not apply to transmission of news by multiple address from the United States to foreign countries. It remains to be seen whether the press associations will have the sustained incentive for extending their services to the backward and relatively less profitable areas, as the British and others are doing.

If they do not do so, agencies must be created which will. The United States cannot afford to take second place in this kind of service. It is at once the right and the duty of a people fated to play a leading role to tell its own story in its own way. But international understanding requires much more than that the American people tell their story fully and fairly. What is needed is a dozen or more reliable news agencies, each checking the others, and all vying for the respect of newspapers and readers everywhere—in short, a global revaluation of the currency of truthful reporting.

American press associations have built a tradition of relative independence. They have resisted alliances with governments. They see themselves increasingly as "objective" purveyors of the reality of events. More, perhaps, than any agencies of international news exchange, they are qualified to earn a place with the peoples of other lands as reliable, accurate sources of reporting the day's events, not only from and to the United States but also from one foreign country to another. As such, they are in a position to serve as practical agents of international understanding, should they elect to follow this course.

IV. THE PRESS AND THE MERGER

The problem of adequate physical facilities for the newer tasks of press transmission raises a third important question in planning postwar international telecommunications—one that has only recently been given the attention it deserves. This is the question of whether all press physical facilities—point-to-point as well as multiple address, and specifically Press Wireless—should be included in any merger.

The case for exemption has been put by Press Wireless and seems to be supported almost unanimously by the newspaper industry. The basis for the request lies in the history and special functions of press communications in relation to general telecommunications carriers.

Press Wireless, Incorporated was a direct attempt by the newspapers to meet the bad service and high rates of the commercial carriers by organizing a company to serve the press directly and solely. The newspapers had sought, at first, to solve their problem by creating individual communications agencies, but the Federal Radio Commission (forerunner of F.C.C.), faced even then with the need to conserve short-wave frequencies, insisted on the formation of a single company. The effect of the new carrier on press rates was almost immediate. Within a short time the rates were cut from 50 to 80 per cent. Service was improved by the competitor and the competition alike. An example of the results of having a carrier specifically devoted to press needs has been the mobile press transmitters put into effective use by Press Wireless on the battlefronts in Europe and the Pacific. Mackay, which got the nod in Algiers, and R.C.A.C., first to go into Italy, did not serve the press so well.

As a strenuous competitor for a profitable segment of the commercial carriers' business, Press Wireless in its early years had difficulty in purchasing equipment from those companies which engaged in manufacturing as well as communication. As a result, Press Wireless put its profits into research and has an excellent record in initiating technological improvements. These include not only multiple-address transmission but also four-color facsimile, reliable radioprinter reception, a frequency-shift principle which increases reception quality in geometric ratio as power is increased arithmetically, and a carrier-shift principle which makes it possible to broadcast voice or facsimile simultaneously with dot-dash, from the same transmitter, using the same frequency.

The argument for exemption from merger is based on the special needs and requirements of the press for high priority in transmission of press material and low transmission rates. The press experience, before Press Wireless came into being, was that the less profitable (per word) press business was neglected on behalf of commercial clients and high-priority government business. The newspapers believe that their own company can serve them better and cheaper. Not emphasized in public discussion but existing as a real motive for exemption is the press desire not to be tied in with a merger which is partly a cable operation and which has to share the burden of higher cable costs. The newspapers have sought to create the impression that Press Wireless, included in a total merger, would, for the first time, be subject to governmental regulation and that this would interfere with "freedom of the press." Actually, Press Wireless is now legally a public utility, under strict governmental regulation as to rates and services; in a merger it would not be in a different category. But despite such irrelevancies, the press case for exemption or separate treatment is a good one.

Advocates of incorporating Press Wireless in a merger do so on the ground that the inclusive, vastly extended network of the merged company would place at the disposal of the press a more efficient total instrument of rapid global communication than could possibly be built up independently. There is also the ever present need to economize frequencies and the belief that by inclusive merger the fullest use of each assigned frequency would be made. Additional argument for including press-transmission facilities in a merger may be adduced from the 1945 Bermuda telecommunications conference of British and American governments. There the British, looking forward to a unified governmental telecommunications system, probably under the Post Office, proposed general adoption of the British Empire penny-rate ceiling for press material. This was rejected by the Americans on the ground that an independent agency such as Press Wireless cannot operate on a penny rate—that such a low rate implies, in fact, a subsidy of press traffic by other traffic. If a press-rate subsidy is considered sound public policy, it requires a merger of press with other facilities.

But the advocates of inclusion are beginning to recognize the need for autonomy of press facilities within the merger—separate physical facilities and a separate rate structure. The differences between the advocates of exemption and inclusion, therefore, are not great.

It would seem to us that if adequate frequencies can be found, it would be desirable to permit the maintenance of an independent press communications agency. In allowing such exemption, the statute should clearly specify that Press Wireless (or whatever entity may succeed to it) should be broadly inclusive in its membership—open to all types of press users, including radio broadcasting companies and magazines; that its surplus should be used mainly for research and development rather than distributed as dividends; and that it should remain clearly under federal regulatory control as to rates and service, including power of the federal agency to require extensions of service. By such regulation the government may be able to insure the global coverage by multiple-address newscasts which is so desirable from a social point of view.

Our preference for independence at this time is based principally on the idea that, with press communication entering on a period of expansion involving the broadcast mechanism, it can develop more quickly and surely by itself than only as part of a large organization devoted principally to other purposes.

Also, there would seem to be an obvious advantage in the maintenance of competition for the press business between Press Wireless and the merged corporation. The merged company would, of course, be permitted to carry press material at press rates. It would offer point-to-point facilities in some instances not available through Press Wireless. The larger unit might also develop multiple-address facilities in competition with Press Wireless. If the Mackay multiple-address facilities are developed, they would be ready at hand in the merged entity for this purpose. Hence, if the advantages of handling press materials as part of a merger proved after actual experience to be very real, the separate company would lose its reason for being and drop out of existence within a few years. In the meantime, the maintenance of a separate press entity appears to offer the best insurance against hasty decisions which might be regretted later. Indeed, only by exempting Press Wireless from the merger and seeing to it that the merger offers identical facilities can the opponents of exempting Press Wireless prove their case by actual comparative experience.

V. VOICE BROADCASTING

International voice broadcasting from the United States has been all but left out of the picture in planning the postwar telecommunications structure. Yet as a means of direct, widespread diffusion of news and information throughout the world, and especially from a government or people of one country to the people of another, voice broadcasting has come to stay.

Developed in the thirties by European countries and Japan as a cultural link with imperial possessions or as a means of propaganda, it was still mainly a laboratory project for American broadcasting companies. Recognizing that the medium might never have more than limited appeal to advertisers and that they therefore would have to provide most of the cost indefinitely, the National Broadcasting Company and the Columbia Broadcasting System initiated only modest experiments. General Electric, Westinghouse, and Crosley, which had radio equipment to sell, looked on short-wave broadcasting as a logical medium for a limited amount of institutional or prestige advertising. Later, Associated Broadcasters, Incorporated, a West Coast concern, staked out a small Latin-American market. Of the seven so-called "licensees" who were engaged in direct international voice broadcasting from the United States on Pearl Harbor Day, only the World Wide Broadcasting Company has been able to attract enough outside money to cover its costs. This it did by setting up a foundation to conduct a "world university of the air."

With this country's entry into the war, the government, in the form of the Coordinator of Information (later the Overseas Branch of the Office of War Information) and the Coordinator of Inter-American Affairs (later the Office of Inter-American Affairs), stepped in as adviser and monetary angel. A year later O.W.I. and C.I.A.A. took over the seven licensees' thirteen transmitters. Since that time the government has built, in the United States alone, nineteen new transmitters, contributed most of the money for another three, and encouraged the industry to build five with its own money. Most were built on properties of the licensees, and the contracts provided for return of the privately owned transmitters and for purchase of government-owned transmitters at the highest bid or, if no bids are received, by paying cost less 12½ per cent annual depreciation.

But the government did more. It developed short-wave broadcasting from a plaything involving three or four hours' programming a day in half-a-dozen languages to a few areas in Europe and Latin America into a serious business, involving round-the-clock programming in 40–45 languages to literally every part of the globe. It developed the use of automatic relay points such as ABSIE in the British Isles, Radio Luxembourg, Radio Algiers, Radio Bari, and stations in Honolulu, Australia, and Manila, without which direct short-wave from America could not have reached around the world. Plugging away for nearly three years, O.W.I. and O.I.A.A. made the "Voice of America" an indispensable medium of information in many parts of the world, at a cost, exclusive of physical facilities, of $2,000,000–$4,000,000 a year.

As indicated above, the International Broadcasting Subcommittee of the Special Committee on Communications did not produce any definite plan for postwar short-wave broadcasting from this country. The seven pre-war licensees have indicated that they wish to continue, but have not agreed on a common plan as to how they would do so. The dilemma is clear: other governments have developed and will continue after the war to maintain extensive international programs at public expense; the United States during the war developed an equally extensive international program; there seems to be a general feeling that the government program should not continue under government direction; commercial broadcasters who maintain domestic programs by advertising cannot see any way of maintaining an extensive and dignified short-wave program by the same means.

Clearly, it is a case in which the social need for international exchange of information by direct voice broadcast cannot be filled by commercial agencies acting alone. Either government operation or government subsidy of some sort is indicated. The war experience with an extensive short-wave program indicates a necessary over-all arrangement of frequencies and equipment which precludes any attempt to restore individual, competing units for overseas broadcasts. A single, unified organization of physical facilities is required. The simplest means of furnishing these facilities would be for the federal government to organize a government corporation to operate its existing facilities for the use of a nongovernmental association of broadcasters, at rental so low as to constitute, in fact, a substantial subsidy to whatever agency or corporate group undertakes to continue direct international broadcasting from the United States. Government aid through operation of the physical transmission facilities only does not carry the responsibilities or dangers of direct government responsibility for programming and is to be preferred to any other proposal yet made.

For effective short-wave broadcasting to Europe and Asia, the same automatic relay points are necessary as for multiple-address press transmissions. These should be secured for both purposes. Indeed, there might be real economy in uniting these two facilities in the same operation. The wisdom of two-in-one operation does not rest upon the early perfection of carrier-shift transmission. The probabilities are that nothing like the thirty-nine powerful transmitters now used for direct short-wave broadcasting from the United States will be needed for that purpose after the war. It is doubtful whether any one of them will be so used more than four to six hours a day. The arguments for keeping them and their technical staffs busy full time by transmitting multiple-address newscasts as well as voice broadcasts are therefore obvious.

VI. FORM OF THE MERGER

The form that any telecommunications merger will take should be determined in large part by the major factors described above: i.e., amortization of the cables; provision for global coverage by multiple-address newscasts; strict autonomy or independence of an inclusive press communications entity; adequate provision for international voice broadcasting through continued government provision of unified physical facilities for voice broadcasts; definite planning for automatic relay stations for multiple-address press and short-wave voice broadcasts from the United States to Europe, Africa, and Asia.

There are at least two other factors which need to be taken into account in any merger of facilities. Neither is related to our primary concern with universal, cheap, and efficient exchange of news and information. Neither, however, in any way suggests any contrary formula for telecommunications organization. One is the need to maintain for purposes of military contingency an efficient, widespread, global telecommunications network, to be turned to instant military use in case of war or threat of war. The second factor is the obvious commercial desirability of having a cheap and efficient global network for business and personal messages. Inevitably, the United States, along with Great Britain, has the existing equipment not only to serve ourselves but, in competition with other national systems, to carry a large part of the world's rapid communications also. If we follow the practice of serving actually as an international common carrier, without discrimination in rates or services between the nationals of any country, our carrier will be of general benefit to the world's trade and intercourse.

What form of merger do all these considerations dictate? The public defense of the various proposals made by government officials tends to suggest the opposition of monopoly and competition—an unreal contrast. Merger, as it has been proposed, does not mean monopoly, with absence of the incentives of competition. It is a unification of certain facilities which leaves a very real competition still in full play. On the other hand, absence of merger does not mean free competition. Government regulation of rates and services of existing companies is now in force. Its effect is to maintain rates at levels designed to preserve the less efficient units.

It is possible to gain many of the advantages of unified operation of facilities and at the same time to retain competition in service and efficiency. If we presume that the cable and radiotelegraph companies are merged into a single concern, with Press Wireless exempt from such a merger, the American people would have two choices and the press three choices for rapid communication with other countries.

First would be a global point-to-point cable and wireless network connected at the water's edge with a single domestic telegraph network. Second would be a global interconnecting airmail service. Third would be a specialized press service operating to and from the United States. No one of these three competing companies would duplicate the facilities of the others to any great extent. Bad service or high rates on one would shift press traffic to another. Except for air mail, the two would in many foreign places be in direct competition with foreign facilities of like kind. Thus, such merger as has been suggested does not eliminate the value of competition in service.

The advantages of unification of radiotelegraph and cable facilities are of real importance. Frequencies to be shared internationally are at the moment scarce. A cable-wireless company, by using its existing cable capacity to the full, would relieve the wireless load as much as possible. Moreover, the creation of a diversified and widespread cable and wireless network would provide a maximum of safety for use of alternative routes during interruptions and would distribute peak loads so that speed would be maintained. Patents now owned by the several constituent companies would be pooled, and duplicate facilities would be eliminated. In establishing contractual relations with foreign land-line and wireless companies, the American cable-wireless carrier would speak with unity. An integrated network would be in full operation in case of military need. Thus, from a technological point of view, the advantages of cable and wireless unification seem clear.

The question as to the inclusion of United States international radiotelephone facilities in the merged network is not directly relevant to the primary problem of seeking cheap, fast, universal, nondiscriminatory transmission of press material. On both technical and economic grounds, there are arguments both ways on this particular issue. On behalf of merger are the advantages cited above of fuller use of available short-wave frequencies, availability of alternative routes during interruptions and to distribute peak loads, unity in foreign rates negotiations, and integration for unified operation in case of military need. These arguments, however, are not so forceful in the case of radiotelephone as in the cases of cables and wireless telegraph. A written message from the point of origin is completely and quickly available for transmission interchangeably by cable or radiotelegraph. A telephone message is a different communication process: oral rather than written, a two-way exchange rather than one way.

Furthermore, our domestic organization of telephone and telegraph implies a monopoly or near-monopoly for each one. With a merger of radiotelegraph and cable only, the individual customer in sending messages abroad would have a simple choice of three means. He could write an air-mail letter and drop it in the nearest post box to be sent to any point in the world. He could go to the nearest Western Union office and send a written message to any part of the world. He could take down his telephone receiver and talk directly to someone halfway around the world. These are three different kinds of rapid communication; the news reporter could sit at the teletypewriter and send his message by a fourth route also—Press Wireless, Incorporated. The sender would choose one or the other on the basis of how quickly he wished to transmit his message, how much he wished to say, how immediately he wished an answer. Whereas radiotelephone and radiotelegraph have real advantages in common use of facilities, they do operate separately to a great degree from a technical point of view and have separate rate systems. Finally, there is the clear advantage, other things being nearly equal, in retaining competition in service.

For the immediate future, then, while a merged radiotelegraph and cable company is getting under way and perfecting its management and while radiotelephony is still in an early stage of its technical development, it would seem prudent to postpone the inclusion of the radiotelephone in any merger. If, later, technical consideration should call for an opposite conclusion, it would in no way affect the general pattern of our recommendations made primarily in the interest of press communications.

As to the form of ownership which the merged company should take, the choice is between a government corporation operated at cost solely in the public interest and a private corporation strictly and extensively regulated by the federal government in the public interest. Most of the major factors mentioned above would seem to be best taken into account by a new corporation issuing stock to the present owners, including the government, to represent the value of the contributed plant and equipment in each case, scaling down, however, the cable valuation to represent more nearly the present actual value of the cable investment. In such a plan of mixed stock ownership, the government should hold the majority of the total stock and should have an equivalent majority of the board of directors. The government members appointed by the President should be chosen to represent not only the military interests in the merged network but also the international interest in global coverage by press and radio. With such a corporation clearly controlled in the public interest, there should be included a unified network of voice broadcast and multiple-address press transmitters, with the purchase and installation of the necessary automatic relay stations for coverage of the European and Asiatic regions. In this way the nonprofit but socially valuable facilities for international communication would be provided simply by having the more profitable parts of the global network make up for any operating losses. It is in this way under our Post Office that New York–Chicago–Philadelphia–Boston mail revenues pay for rural free delivery in Alaska.

The merger would make possible, for the first time, unified ownership and operation of facilities which it is advantageous to integrate from an economic point of view and perfectly feasible to integrate from a technical standpoint but which are not now unified. This is especially true of short-wave broadcast transmitters and relay stations to be used both for voice broadcasts and for multiple-address newscasts. Both are marginal operations at present from a financial point of view. Both require broad-beam channels. Operated under the same management, they would make the fullest and most economical use of frequencies and equipment. Operated as part of a general telecommunications merger, the cost of their promotion period in reaching less thickly settled areas would be borne by the larger returns from trunk-line business between capitals.

The government-controlled corporation would not be a monopoly. A press entity and probably a radiotelephone entity would exist outside the merger. Competition between the three services and air mail would continue.

If political or other considerations prevent the organization of such a government corporation, the next best solution would seem to be a merger of radiotelegraph and cable companies under private ownership but with strict government regulation as to rates and service. Such an arrangement, however, would probably preclude the inclusion of the international voice broadcast and multiple-address newscast transmitters, for the reason that a private corporation could not easily be required to furnish the voice-broadcast and multiple-address newscast facilities at a loss or without profit. These latter should then be reserved by the government, to be operated in common as a small government corporation without profit.

The third and least desirable alternative would be the organization of a nongovernmental corporation, as suggested above, with provision for multiple-address and voice-broadcast functions either in the exempted Press Wireless entity, entirely in the merged corporation, or both, with specific statutory power vested in the F.C.C. to regulate multiple-address and voice-broadcast rates and service so as to require adequate coverage of backward areas.

VII. SUMMARY

In summary, then, the most desirable program to provide physical facilities and operating mechanisms for communication of words and images across national borders as abundantly, as cheaply, as quickly, and as efficiently, and over as wide an area, as possible, seems to be that:

1. *All United States cable and radiotelegraph companies, with exceptions to be noted below, be merged, voluntarily if possible (and if not possible, by congressional act) and joined with government facilities not needed for direct military purposes to establish a global telecommunications network, to handle commercial, military, diplomatic, press, and voice-broadcasting traffic.*

2. *Exemption from the merger be allowed for a single telecommunications corporation devoted entirely to the transmission of press matter, provided that such corporation maintain membership rules to provide inclusion of all bona fide press users, including newspapers, press associations, magazines, and radio broadcasting companies, and with voting arrangements calculated to distribute control fairly among these different users; and that if no such telecommunications corporation applies for the privilege of exemption, there be made specific regulations in the merged corporation for autonomous physical and financial operation of press transmission facilities.*

3. *Exemption from compulsory merger be granted for the present also to existing radiotelephone facilities.*

4. *In the organization of the merged corporation definite provision be made for a revaluation of the cable company investments so that their valuation will be in close relation to present actual capital value.*

5. *Definite provision for regulation of the merged corporation in the public interest be made either by government ownership of a majority of the stock in the merged company, with consequent majority membership on the board of directors, and with statutory limitation of dividends of the stock privately held in the merged corporation; or by private ownership of all stock in the merged*

corporation, with specific power of comprehensive regulation of rates and service, including extension of service in the public interest, assigned to the federal regulatory authority.

6. *By government control of policy or by governmental regulation as defined above, positive steps be taken to provide physical facilities for multiple-address, dot-dash, and facsimile (including radiophoto) wireless transmission and direct international voice broadcasting, so that these facilities, together with facilities separately furnished by the press facilities corporation, will cover every habitable part of the world.*

7. *Definite arrangements be made to acquire automatic relay stations for multiple-address newscasts and short-wave broadcasts from the United States to Europe and Asia for the use of United States public or private corporations authorized to carry on such services.*

INTERNATIONAL REGULATION

The organization and regulation of a world telecommunications network is not a task which can be accomplished by our government and our industries acting alone. At three points, especially, agreements between governments are necessary. First is the allocation of the short-wave frequencies so that the traffic initiated at different points on the earth's surface can assume an orderly pattern and not be involved in hopeless snarls of interference. Second is the making of rate agreements for commercial traffic running across national borders and involving the rate-making authority of two or more nations.[6] Third is the need of nations without widespread colonial possessions to secure relay stations for multiple-address newscasting and voice broadcasting.

The first need for international agreement—that of allocating frequencies—has been recognized as a necessity since radio short waves began to be used seriously in Europe. As early as 1932, the

[6] A commercial telecommunications rate of this kind is assessed in three parts: i.e., the cost of service at the point of origin, the cost of transmission, and the cost of receipt and delivery at the point of destination. The regulatory agency of any one national system can, at most, legally control the assessment of costs at one end only. The result is a great deal of maneuvering, discrimination, and inconsistency in the international telecommunications rate structure.

United States joined with the European and other national states at Madrid in adhering to the Radio Regulations Section of the International Telecommunications Convention. This section made an allocation of the short-wave frequencies for distress signals, commercial point-to-point radiotelegraph, and voice broadcasting between the various interested countries. The Convention was revised at a conference in Cairo in 1938, and another conference is planned for 1946. In addition, an American Hemisphere Conference to revise regional frequency allocations and other regulations was held in September, 1945.

Although these conferences have been successful in reaching agreements for division of the high-frequency bands used for long-distance communication and in setting up a bureau in Berne for keeping a record of frequencies actually being used under the Convention, the administrative machinery for maintenance of the agreements in actual operation is quite inadequate. Our State Department, backed by the F.C.C. and other federal agencies, is planning to propose at the next conference a more workable minimum of international machinery, including a frequency registration board to keep a current record of all frequencies used, to notify offending parties of violation of frequency assignments, and to utilize national monitoring units, such as that maintained in the United States by the F.C.C., to report actual infringements in practice. These are the first steps in what must increasingly be an area for international administration, with as much authority as is exercised in the area of communicable diseases or communication by mail.

In the matter of international machinery for regulation of radiotelegraph, radiotelephone, and cable rates, the United States has hitherto refused to join as a partner with other countries. The International Telegraph and International Telephone Sections of the Telecommunications Union grew out of an International Telegraph Union organized in Europe during the late nineteenth century. The United States has never joined it. *The United States should cooperate as far as possible with the rate-regulation structures made by the Telecommunications Union.* The problem of rates is admittedly complex, but it admits of great simplification over the present system. In point-to-point traffic, where the word is the unit of charge, there may be great merit in the uniform-rate principle which has been such an unqualified success in national postal systems and in the International Postal Union. It has also been instituted by the British Cable and Wireless, Limited, with a uniform press rate for the whole of the British Empire. It is especially appropriate as a tariff principle for radiotelegraph and radiotelephone, in which the capital and operating costs are practically the same for short and long distances through the ether. The recent Bermuda Anglo-American conference made an important beginning both in eliminating discrimination through exclusive arrangements for direct communication between either country and other foreign countries and in establishing uniform, lowered ceiling rates for both commercial and press international traffic. It furnishes a simple pattern for negotiating international agreements designed to furnish cheap, universal, nondiscriminatory commercial telecommunication around the world.

The matter of relay points is one in which the United States has a special concern. The securing of two or three such points on foreign soil will probably remain for the present a matter of bilateral arrangement between our government and the sovereign owner of the territory we wish to lease. Suggestions have been made, however, that the matter of relay points and the creation of an international pattern for short-wave broadcasting from internationally controlled, powerful voice-broadcast transmitters located at a half-dozen points around the globe be seriously considered as an objective by the International Telecommunications Union. From a long-term point of view, this seems to be a sound proposal. When the United Nations Organization moves into permanent quarters, a revival and development of the international radio station started at Geneva in the thirties, carrying international news by means of a powerful transmitter on assigned short wave, would seem a highly desirable communications instrument for the activities of the Organization's councils, commissions, and committees—perhaps for other purposes.

So much for physical facilities. For the most part, they already exist, and the problem is therefore simply to determine how to use them most effectively. What of the instruments that would utilize not only wireless in all its amazing new forms but also the postwar air lines that already loom as competitors of telecommunications even in terms of speed? Do they also, for the most part, already exist? Are there barriers other than the lack of cheap, efficient transmission facilities that could limit their effectiveness?

4

MERCHANTS OF WORDS AND IMAGES

THANKS to the war, the world never had so many instruments which can be used for improving understanding among peoples as it has today. The unprecedented demand for news, background, and interpretation has brought new information agencies into the field and spurred old ones into expanding not only their services but also their concepts of the work to be done. Press associations, which before the war were interested primarily in bringing news of the world to their countries, are now concentrating on selling news throughout the world. Book publishers, who formerly wrote off foreign sales as a "2 per cent nuisance," now regard themselves as vital instruments of international understanding. In a dozen countries, flourishing motion-picture industries are preparing to challenge Hollywood's long-time supremacy —and, in consequence, Hollywood shows signs of being aware that it must do a better job in the export market. The international circulation of finished newspapers and magazines, once regarded as an impractical dream, has become an accomplished fact. Although the future pattern of international voice broadcasting at the moment is less clear, the next decade is certain to witness the linking of the remotest areas of the world through this modern medium.

In mass communication, information is circulated internationally in three forms: as raw material, as semifinished goods, and as finished product. Raw material may be described as the dispatches of foreign correspondents to their home newspapers and magazines, the pictures of still photographers and newsreel cameramen, the reports of radio newsmen broadcast to their compatriots by their home broadcasting stations or networks, and the materials out of which authors write books and free-lance magazine articles. Semifinished goods may be described as regular press association and picture-feature syndicate services, which the recipient may use in full, cut, combine with material from other sources, or discard. Finished products include books, magazines, newspapers, motion pictures, and direct country-to-country radio broadcasts reaching the consumer in final, unchangeable form.

Obviously, in the three cases the barriers encountered are quite different, both as to form and as to significance. We may agree with alacrity that everyone is entitled to the raw materials of information. We may go a step further and say that, for the sake of obvious economies of effort and expense to the editor and radio-station manager, everyone who wants them should have unhampered access to semifinished goods. But we may hesitate to insist that any people has a right to flood other peoples with finished products, for it is a fact that where no editor can intervene between his compatriots and information-suppliers in other lands to make comprehensible what would otherwise be incomprehensible and to clothe the isolated incident in its historic context, the effect may be to produce misunderstanding rather than understanding; and that where no editor can detect and reject sheer propaganda, governments may be tempted to substitute it for information.

THE NEWS-GATHERERS

It often has been remarked that the interchange of information through mass media will attain its perfect state only when every people is adequately represented throughout the world by competent observers—i.e., when all information starts with imported raw material. Such a system certainly would go far toward checking propaganda, and, assuming an abundance of domestic mass media to air the findings of these observers, most nations probably would subsist very well on nothing but raw material from abroad.

It is interesting to recall that, except for a smattering of books, this is precisely how the world operated until the turn of the century. It is interesting, too, to note the historic sequence in the development of mass media: the coming of new mechanical devices created popular demand for their products rather than the other way around; and government interference with mass media began to assert itself only as the concentration of the means of communication made systematized interference practicable. The first World War began, and the recent war greatly accelerated, a trend away from raw-material imports to the export of finished goods. Doktor Goebbels became the East India Company of our time.

Prior to the invention of printing type, news traveled by word of mouth and by letter, with the choicest bits of court scandal and international intrigue reserved for the safety and embellishment of conversation. The advantages of the confidential courier were preserved long after the coming of the newspaper. In part, this was because editors appreciated that their news-gatherers were protected in the disguise of a bank clerk or a ship's captain. In part, it was because the original purchaser of the news was not an editor at all but an enterprising businessman who let the editor have it only when he could extract no further profit from its exclusiveness. In any event, although governments created the most important news, they could not control it in a society in which every other traveler might be a part-time reporter.

I. REUTER, THE PRESS ASSOCIATIONS, AND THE CARTEL

Among the most enterprising businessmen of the pretelegraph period in Europe were the Fuggers and later the Rothschilds, who had discovered early that palace-scullery gossip could sometimes be turned to account in the money mart. In the 1840's a no less enterprising German, named Paul Julius Reuter, found that homing pigeons could beat the Rothschilds' couriers. In 1851, on the advice of the Rothschilds, Reuter took his pigeons to London, where he used them to link the newfangled telegraph lines that could span everything in Europe but the Skagerrak and the English Channel.

Three things immediately became apparent to Reuter: (1) copper wire was going to revolutionize and standardize the whole news-gathering operation; (2) because this would give governments the opportunity to interfere with what was said, the wise news merchant would seek to make himself a partner and confidant of government; and (3) newspapers were becoming so numerous and so bulky that they were better wordage-volume customers than brokerage houses. Armed with such wisdom, Reuter approached the *Times* with a proposition to furnish English newspapers with Continental coverage by his staff of foreign observers. The *Times* was skeptical, but the editor of the *Advertizer* closed a shrewd bargain with him.

Within twelve months Reuter was serving a dozen newspapers in the British Isles and making money at it. But his sights were aimed higher: If the government would permit him to use the new submarine cables that were beginning to link the empire's outposts, the global news service he proposed to develop would cement British ties and help to fill the holds of British merchantmen. He may have added, as an afterthought, that such a plan already had occurred to a Frenchman named Havas.

In any event the British government was quick to see the point. Reuter became a British citizen, a trusted servant without portfolio. Needless to add, Reuter's news service was careful to say at crucial points what the British government wished it to say.

Meantime, Havas, who had been rounding up Continental news for French newspapers since 1835, was also dreaming of world empire. Havas fought Reuter for a year, but the favorite of Westminster held the high trumps—the cables. Then as now, limited facilities argued limited competition. So Havas persuaded Wolff, a German agency founded in 1849, that prudence dictated dividing the world into three parts. Reuter got the British empire, North America, a number of "suzerain" states along the Mediterranean-Suez lifeline, and most of Asia; Havas got the French empire, southwestern Europe, South America, and parts of Africa; Wolff got what was left in Europe, including Austria-Hungary, Scandinavia, and the Slav states.

Reuter soon discovered that he was in for trouble in the United States, where a number of newspaper publishers in 1848 had decided to husband their limited facilities by organizing a co-operative news-gathering agency which they styled the "Associated Press." The British government did not want trouble with America over anything touching United States sovereignty so closely and for such relatively small stakes; so Reuter convinced Havas that the original partners would benefit by letting A.P. into the cartel, since its inclusion would enable them to cover the news of the distant republic without spending a farthing. Even so, A.P. was not formally admitted until 1887.

During the succeeding years there were changes and modifications of the original four-trust agreement. Smaller news agencies, like Italy's Stefani and Belgium's Belga, sprang up, only to be forced to become satellites of Reuter or Havas. Here and there, as in the Caribbean and in Central America, Reuter and Havas agreed to share a market. A.P. was confined to continental United States until after the turn of the century, when it was permitted to venture into Canada and Mexico, and, toward the close of the first World War, into Central and South America. Thus it was that, from 1858 to the first World War, reporting, save in the United States, was never quite free of the taint of government propaganda.

A good many editors, particularly in America, writhed in their strait jackets. They themselves traveled abroad enough to know that they were not getting the facts. Some of the more enterprising, like James Gordon Bennett the elder, sought to gain a measure of independence from the cartel by sending special correspondents to roam the world, as the pre-Reuter couriers had done and as the individual British newspaper correspondents did. A.P. itself was able to place some of its correspondents in foreign capitals with the right of filing their reports directly to the United States. But it was not until a new enlargement of the telecommunications bottleneck coincided with the development of cheap newsprint and high-speed presses to focus a widespread demand for better news coverage that the cartel got its first serious warning of doom.

The break came during the first decade of the present century. The Commercial Cable Company was challenging the Western Union–British stranglehold on the Atlantic cables and preparing to buy into the new Pacific links. Radiotelegraphy was blossoming as a cheap alternative carrier, capable of carrying many thousands of words a day. The improved Hoe high-speed rotary press was shifting the balance of interest to afternoon newspapers, with their multiple split-second editions for street sales. Among the most vigorous of these afternoon papers were those of the midwestern and far western chains owned by the Scripps family, which, because of A.P.'s exclusive-franchise agreements, could not buy that agency's service. In 1907 the Scripps organized the United Press Associations.

U.P. soon was joined in the anticartel fight by Hearst's International News Service. By 1914, noncartel correspondents dotted the globe, for U.P. and I.N.S. were not alone. Although for political reasons they would not formally break with the monopoly, venturesome British, Dutch, French, Scandinavian, and Japanese editors could and did send their own reporters forth to "supplement" the cartel's coverage. In Canada, Australia, and Japan cooperative news associations were formed, with the partial object of eliminating governmental dominance.

By dint of considerable energy and some good luck, U.P. by 1920 had broken the cartel front at what had been regarded as its strongest point: the non–United States news-buying market. A fortuitous friendship between a U.P. executive and the owners of *La Prensa* of Buenos Aires led, despite Havas' protests, to U.P. contracts with a number of Latin-American newspapers. At about the same time, A.P. extended its membership to include a number of leading South and Central American newspapers. And the forthright demand of several English provincial newspapers for something better than Reuter resulted in the formation of British United Press, an entirely British-owned association having close ties with U. P., with which it exchanged news items.

II. DIVERSIFICATION IN FOREIGN NEWSGATHERING

Although Germany's defeat in 1918 gave Wolff's share of the cartel to Havas and Reuter, the old arrangement was finished. Struggling new agencies like Exchange Telegraph in England and

Agence Radio in France had followed the U.P.–I.N.S. example. One-paper special correspondents were becoming commonplace in the world's principal cities. Soon their newspapers, singly or in groups, organized syndicates to sell their global coverage to less venturesome editors. Thus, such newspapers as the *London Daily Mail,* the *London Daily Express,* the *Manchester Guardian,* the *Stockholm Tidningens,* the *Berliner Tageblatt,* the *Züricher Zeitung, La Prensa* and *Nación* of Buenos Aires, the *Frankfurter Zeitung,* the *Petit Parisien,* the *Tokyo Nippon Dempo,* the *Philadelphia Public Ledger,* the *New York Evening Post,* the *New York World,* the *New York Herald Tribune,* the *New York Times,* and the *Chicago Daily News* branched out as small press associations in the news-selling, as well as the news-gathering, market.

During the late twenties and early thirties, foreign coverage made rapid strides both in the number of observers roaming the world and in the quality of the best of them. Magazine correspondents joined the ranks of newspapermen. As the importance of pictures increased, news photographers and newsreel cameramen began to apply for admission to the correspondents' corps. In the late thirties, radio newsmen and commentators added their eyes and voices.

The very rapid development of wireless and aviation had made possible a flow of words and pictures such as Paul Julius Reuter had never envisioned. The expansion in size and scope of existing periodicals and the creation of many new ones offered a ready outlet for the increased flow. The best of the correspondents departed from time-honored press association methods and began to dig deeply into the social patterns of the countries to which they were assigned. The invention of the "candid" camera and the perfection of fine-screen photographic printing on improved calendar magazine stock called forth a host of first-class photographers, whose art was brought to the home news desk by wire and wireless photo in a matter of minutes. Better book publishing and merchandising methods invited those who roamed the world in search of knowledge to put between covers the best of what they found.

Again, as in Reuter's time, newer and better facilities inspired newer and better uses of the means of international communication; newer and better uses spurred a popular demand for their continuance and improvement. The independent observer and the wireless telegraph had outmoded Reuter's methods, just as Reuter's news network and the cable had outmoded the methods of his predecessors. In the early thirties, A.P. broke away completely from the cartel. In 1940 Havas vanished with the French armies. A year later, British newspaper proprietors took over Reuter. In 1942 Mussolini's puppet, Stefani, disappeared, to be succeeded by the Agenzia Nazionale Stampa Associata, modeled along the lines of A.P. and the new Reuter; and the co-operative association, Agence France Presse, rose from the ruins of the venal Havas. The fall of Deutsche Nachrichten Buro and the Japanese Domei in 1945 left only Spain's E.F.E. and the Russian agency Tass in the field of openly government-controlled news services.

There is every reason to suppose that the development of wireless multiple-address press and voice broadcasting, together capable of carrying tens of thousands of words and scores of pictures daily to literally every corner of the globe at a fraction of a cent a word, will encourage a quantitative flow of information such as the world has never known. It is now possible, mechanically at least, for any publication to receive the equivalent of a hundred thousand words of foreign news daily. The ideal of trained observers roaming the universe, writing freely and fully of what they see and feel, presses impatiently against political barriers which, ironically, bid fair to stifle the flow of information in some areas at the precise moment that science has elected to make the widest flow physically practicable. Will the "irresistible" ideal shatter against the "immovable" barriers? There will be times in the near future when it will seem to in certain areas. But there will be more times and more areas where the barriers will give way. As with any other, this particular ideal will prevail to the extent that men persist through disappointment and compromise.

What are the artificial barriers that impede the flow across national borders of informational raw materials? The shortcomings of the present telecommunications systems have been stressed. Obviously, the most reliable news service in the world cannot reach those who are not reached by cable or wireless; the finest magazines and books and pictures cannot reach those who are not reached by fast plane.

Virtually every nation now forbids foreign radiotelegraph companies the right to maintain their own receiving facilities within its borders. The result is that local companies, usually government owned or controlled, supply reception and internal distribution facilities at whatever rates they can command, with further delays in transmission. Although this situation does not involve multiple-address newscasts or shortwave voice broadcasts (except for automatic relay points) and although radiotelephone has worked out relatively satisfactory reciprocal arrangements for international traffic, it is a serious handicap not only to "trunk-line" news transmissions between two points but also to commercial-message traffic. *What is indicated here is a multilateral agreement, binding all nations to permit authorized wireless telegraph and cable companies (and airlines as well) to maintain suitable terminal facilities wherever they are required, subject only to the regulations binding domestic companies, or to maintain nondiscriminatory two-way connections between its own and foreign companies, as has been developed for wireless telephony.* The Bermuda agreements marked a step in this direction.

The need for automatic wireless relay points has been mentioned. These could be obtained through year-to-year leasing of foreign-owned facilities. But wartime experience with this device has shown that long-time control of the relay transmitters by the sender is the only completely satisfactory solution short of the setting-up of international relay points to be operated under the control of an international telecommunications union. Pending the more ideal solution, which does not appear to be immediately realizable, *a sound proposal would seem to involve bilateral treaties giving those nations which require relay points extra-territorial privileges under long-term lease.*

IV. ACCESS AT THE SOURCE

Meantime, there are other and more serious barriers to the free flow of informational raw materials across national frontiers. Discrimination and censorship are the two broad headings that cover those evils of which foreign correspondents (and natives, too, for that matter) most often complain. What do newspapermen mean by these terms?

In Nazi Germany reporters could not wander about at will, writing of what they saw and felt. Doktor Goebbels and his press section gave them stereotyped handouts, took them on stereotyped trips. The parts of Germany and German-occupied lands that they did not see were the special province not merely of German newsmen but of "reliable" German newsmen. The defeat of Germany brought an end to Goebbels; but correspondents may face precisely the same type of discrimination, in varying degree, for a long time to come in Russia and the Russian "spheres" in Europe and Asia and in Spain, China, various Latin-American countries, Saudi Arabia, and certain parts of the British, French, Belgian, and Netherlands empires.

It is characteristic of the one-party type of government to fear criticism and to make provisions to exclude it, on the pious ground that not all reporters have the mental capacity to criticize fairly. This is the antithesis of the democratic view. Experience in the United States, Canada, the United Kingdom, Australia and New Zealand, France, Belgium, the Netherlands, Denmark, Norway, Sweden, and Switzerland has built up a reassuring body of evidence that unfair critics sooner or later defeat their own purposes. It may be useless to try to convince Russia and the others that this is so. The Russians already have made it clear that they think Americans and Britons are foolish to permit newsmen so much freedom, and they can quote more than one recent instance of our newsmen's harmful irresponsibility. Reminders from friendly British and American newspapermen that secrecy in itself is likely to breed unwarranted suspicion and give rise to imaginative "news stories" about Russia of the familiar type which, in the twenties and thirties, usually bore Riga datelines apparently do not move the Narkomindell.

This is a problem that will have to be faced and solved. For no news coverage that includes only the "official" versions of events in Russia, Poland, Rumania, Bulgaria, Yugoslavia, Spain, China, Argentina, Iran, Syria and the Lebanon, Palestine, Arabia, Algeria, Tunisia, Morocco, French Equatorial Africa, the Congo, British India, the Malay States, the Netherlands Indies, and Indo-China can pretend to the labels "global" or "complete." The problem is not made easier by the fact that everyone knows that the so-called "free-press" countries sometimes preach more zealously than they practice. Britain, for instance, is a conspicuous example of the paradox that distinguishes between the mother-country and its more "backward" dependencies. However much freedom a newspaperman, foreign or native, may enjoy in the British Isles, the moment he sets foot in India he is in another world. The same contrast is noticeable as between metropolitan France and, say, Syria. Even the benevolent and highly democratic Dutch become "security"-minded when a roving newsman debarks at Batavia or Willemstad.

This is not to say that discrimination was never the practice in the mother-countries. In pre-1939 Britain, France, and many another land by tradition devoted to the principle of a free press, it was not uncommon for government officials to show marked preference to a few hand-picked native reporters and even fewer foreigners. The London papers, for instance, felt the pressure of the Chamberlain government during the appeasement period and responded to it to some extent. The Germans made an effort to systematize this practice. Prior to World War I, a Foreign Office press chief named Hammann was permitted to organize a loose affiliation of a few chosen German newspapermen to "interpret" German foreign policy to the German people. The plan does not appear to have been an unqualified success, in part because newspapers which were left out tended to become even more critical and also because the favored few, which happened to include liberal Opposition papers, frequently declined to follow the official line.

The Hammann technique per se will not be tolerated by most newspapermen. But favoritism for individuals (and sometimes even for groups) is widely practiced not only by all governments (including our own) but by private corporations and individuals as well. Actually, newspapermen connive at forming such useful contacts. Indeed, one suspects that the clamor against discrimination of this sort is loudest from those who have been outwitted by it. It becomes impressive only when, as in Russia, it affects all foreigners equally and thus becomes an instrument of anti-internationalism. It is less impressive when newspapermen roll the phrase "equal and unhampered access to all" off their tongues; for every newspaperman must know that equal access would reduce every story to a mass press conference or a mimeographed handout.

What newspapermen really want is what Kent Cooper, executive director of A.P., calls "the right to roam the world at will, writing freely of what they see and feel." This is quite a different thing. It means that what they want is an equal opportunity to use their wits to create *unequal* access. Within that rather broad framework, they want assurances that certain areas will not be open habitually to the few and closed to the many; that news-givers will carefully distinguish between timely news breaks and background material and will confine their special favors to the latter field; and that in the case of "hold-for-release" stories the release date will be scrupulously respected. Newsmen are not always sure even of these things, for in essence these things represent a compromise between the ever warring considerations of security and opportunity that beset anyone engaged in highly competitive private industry. Sorely tempted, a *New York Times*'s Raymond Daniell will join a pool to receive Army favors; a *New York Herald Tribune*'s Theodore Wallen will beseech a Calvin Coolidge to make an "I do not choose to run" news break exclusive; an A.P.'s Edward Kennedy will double-cross his colleagues by breaking a release date. In sum, carte blanche is the maximum that newsmen dream about, equality of opportunity the minimum for which they will settle.

Either is, of course, more difficult of achievement than mere equal access. Both suggest the need for a degree of organized responsibility on the part of newsmen from which they shrink, using the excuse that freedom of the press does not permit of much self-discipline. The apparent paradox has been shrewdly remarked by the Russians; and there is reason to believe that, as long as it persists, it will be a convenient barrier for Moscow to raise against the democracies in the field of international communication. To press for mass interviews and stereotyped handouts, simply because Russia would be more likely to grant such a demand than any other, would be a disservice alike to the correspondents and to their readers. One is tempted to conclude that any deviation from the expressed ultimate goal of "the right to roam the world at will" would lend credence to Moscow's charge that what the newsmen of the democracies are after is simply a chance to make a little more money. A more honorable strategy would appear to be to hold out for the maximum while admonishing the correspondents to grow up to it and, at the same time, frankly recognize that unsettled conditions during the next few years will not be conducive to achievement of the maximum. *This would seem to involve urging a multilateral accord guaranteeing equality of access as between nationals and foreigners*—knowing that the more enterprising in both categories would use that type of equality to get ahead of their fellows.

How, in the meantime, could those who wish to roam the world and write (or photograph) meet the objection of irresponsibility? *One way might be to tighten the foreign correspondents' corps; adopt a code of professional behavior; and require all newsmen, magazine writers, radio people, authors, and photographers to join the corps and observe the code. Appeals from decisions of a government could be taken by the whole corps rather than by an individual, either to the foreign diplomatic corps or to an appropriate unit of the United Nations Economic and Social Council, described later in this report.* A resolute move in this direction might dispose of the contradiction of newsmen asking for group protection while at the same time declining to organize group responsibility.

V. CENSORSHIP

The right to roam the world at will, writing freely, would seem to imply also the right to get what is written to the market. Here we run into another barrier—censorship. Actually, censorship begins at the level of discrimination at the source. But in general usage it is taken to mean the emasculation or total suppression of written and printed matter, pictures and films, and words spoken over a microphone or telephone.

Here, again, the authoritarian powers have been the worst offenders. Before the war, Russia, China, Spain, Portugal, Italy, Germany, Japan, and a number of Latin-American countries openly practiced deletion and suppression. But they did not practice it in the same way. Whereas in Russia correspondents were summoned to discuss cuts and suppressions with the censor who had made them and on occasion were even able to argue him into restoring some of them, in Italy they never knew until they had a chance to check with their home offices from outside what had got through.

More than frank and open censorship itself, newsmen detest the subtler forms. In a sense they have become hardened to a degree of the forthright variety (when a government or corporation official says "Now that's strictly off the record, boys," he automatically becomes a censor); but the honest, conscientious ones will never become resigned to a mixture of censorship, evasion, intimidation, and deceit. They do not like being visited by police who want to "check their papers." They do not like being beaten up in dark alleys. They do not like having their dispatches lie around in telegraph offices until, like ripe fruit, they have lost all market value. They do not like having their houses searched, their families annoyed or terrorized. They do not like clumsy offers of bribes or subtle hints that they might last longer if they were "more correct." But what they like least of all is being forever in the dark, never knowing what the "rules" are, always wondering when they go to work in the morning what they will be able to "get away with" on that particular day.

What can be done to abolish, or at any rate curb, censorship? *A logical first step might be to press for a multilateral agreement pledging the signatories to keep newsmen informed of the rules by which they expect to operate and to abide by them.* If such an agreement could be reached, the climate might encourage *a second and simultaneous step: agreement to limit censorship wherever and as long as it exists to the open deletion or suppression of dispatches in the presence of the writer.* There is little reason to suppose that Russia, which appears to be the key to any multilateral agreement of this sort, would refuse to adhere to either of these provisions. At a favorable moment Moscow might even subscribe to *a third condition: right of appeal by the writer to the correspondents' corps and through it to the United Nations Economic and Social Council.* Meantime, with the ultimate goal of complete abolition of censorship always before us, we could whittle away at the Russian variety, *either through limited multilateral agreement or through a series of bilateral treaties*—although it must be obvious that the former would almost certainly be interpreted by Russia as a revived manifestation of the *cordon sanitaire.*

VI. BARRIERS IN DISTRIBUTION

The right to roam and write would seem to imply not only the right to get to the market what is written but also the right to sell it there without unjust discrimination. This brings us to another barrier: insistence on interposing a middleman (usually government-controlled) between the wholesaler (press association, news-picture agency, or feature syndicate) and the retailer (newspaper, magazine, or radio station). A.P., U.P., I.N.S., Reuter, A.N.S.A., and A.F.P. have recently announced that henceforth they will deal only with reputable individual newspapers, magazines, and radio stations or with bona fide associations of reputable newspapers, magazines, and radio stations. Anesta of the Netherlands, the Swedish Tigningarnas Telegrambyraa, and several other European agencies are expected to fall into line with this stern decision, aimed at preventing the reappearance of anything like Havas or the old Reuter. *Except for bilateral pacts, which would have the effect of blessing such arrangements,* it is difficult to see what might be accomplished by formal convention at this time, since, obviously, those who wish to do business in Russia and China will be obliged to deal with government agencies, as A.P. and Reuter are doing. One factor which ought to do much to discourage middleman monopolies is multiple-address newscasting, which will bring uncensored news to the very borders of monopoly-ridden countries—and even enable the more daring publishers there, by listening in, to check what their governments give them against what the rest of the world is getting.

What of finished products in international communication, as distinguished from the raw material and semifinished goods? How are newspapers, magazines, books, short-wave radio programs, and motion pictures to be circulated across national frontiers in greater numbers? What are the barriers that presently limit this useful flow?

THE PRINTED WORD

The circulation of printed newspapers across national frontiers dates back to the very beginning of newspaperdom, when every ship brought weeks-old copies from foreign ports which were eagerly scanned by government bureaus and liberally borrowed from by editors who had no better way of getting foreign news. Except for limited areas divided by political but not language barriers or as between mother-countries and their colonies, newspapers were not designed for or shipped in sufficient numbers to reach mass audiences directly. With the development of press agencies, editors began to watch for them less eagerly. In the latter part of the nineteenth century a handful of ambitious publishers founded foreign editions, notably James Gordon Bennett's *New York Herald* and Lord Northcliffe's *London Daily Mail,* both in Paris. But these were edited for, and distributed among, nationals of the countries of origin living abroad; and those natives who deciphered them in the hope of improving their knowledge of other peoples were not usually repaid for their pains. After 1900 a number of independent papers like the *Japan Advertiser,* the *Shanghai Post and Mercury,* and the *Manila Times* were launched by and for aliens of the countries in which they were published. Not until the mid-1930's did it occur to governments to try to reach foreign mass audiences directly through the press—and even then the Germans, Italians, Russians, and Japanese preferred the time-honored technique of hiding behind the mastheads of local organs.

The interchange of printed magazines followed much the same pattern. In the 1920's, however, a number of British, American, and German magazine publishers went into the foreign market with the idea of reaching foreigners rather than expatriates. Their publications fell into two classes: women's magazines like the British Amalgamated group's *Woman's World,* which tried a Paris edition; Condé Nast's British and French *Vogue* and French *Jardin des Modes* (German and Spanish *Vogues* were launched in the thirties, quickly scuttled when they did not pan out); Hearst's British editions of *Good Housekeeping, Harper's Bazaar,* and *Connoisseur;* the German *Die Dame,* which circulated widely in Switzerland and eastern Europe—and "pulps" like Macfadden's British, French, German, and Swedish editions of *True Story.*

The war and a number of technical developments have wrought many changes in the techniques of circulating printed newspapers and magazines. Governments were brought into the international publishing business on a scale hitherto undreamed of—thanks, in no small part, to the amazing recent improvements in aviation and offset printing. The German *Signal* at one time boasted a circulation of 7,000,000 outside Germany. Up to 1945 the O.W.I.'s *Victory,* by then jointly sponsored by *Collier's,* had sold 26,000,000 copies in fifteen languages in forty-six countries. The O.I.A.A.'s *En Guardia* had sold 8,000,000 in two languages in sixteen countries. A score of British and Russian publications had reached comparable totals. Moreover, the war (as well as technological improvements) has supplied the spur to a number of private publishers. Thus, at the beginning of 1946, *Reader's Digest* was printing British, Spanish (for Spain), Spanish (for Latin America),

Portuguese (for Portugal), Portuguese (for Brazil), Swedish and Finnish-language editions. *Time, Life,* and *Newsweek* had fourteen, one, and five foreign editions, respectively. *Magazine Digest,* a rapidly growing Canadian monthly, seven-eighths of whose 1,250,000 readers live in the United States, was going forward with plans for several foreign-language editions. The *New York Herald Tribune* and the *London Daily Mail* had revived their Paris editions. The *London Times* was flying a pony edition (greatly reduced in size and printed on thin stock) around the world.

But there were evidences of contraction as well as expansion. The *New York Post,* which entered the Paris afternoon field in August, 1945, was withdrawing for want of American readers. And the *New York Times* apparently had abandoned plans for worldwide facsimile circulation, possibly because its experiments with a facsimile edition at the San Francisco United Nations Conference, while mechanically successful and of great value to the conference, raised a cry of "invasion" from Coast newspapers that caused the A.P. to withdraw the use of its leased wire, over which the edition had been transmitted.

The immediate future for international circulation of newspapers and magazines is far from clear. Government publications (in the United States, at any rate—although the State Department was temporarily continuing *Amerika,* published especially for Russia) did not survive the war. On the other hand, there is an embarrassment of mechanical alternatives which clouds the picture. The sheer bulk and weight of standard-size publications makes their shipment in large quantities by air impracticable. Thus publishers must choose between flying pony editions and printing abroad. Those who elect to print abroad will have a variety of means for getting their copy and pictures to the plant. Whole pages in as many as four colors and in any desired language can be dispatched by wireless in a few minutes. Time, Incorporated, has developed a secret mat of the color and consistency of cellophane, which compresses an entire issue of *Time* or *Life* into a packet which a plane pilot could store in his cap. Printing plates for rotary or flat-bed presses can be pulled with equal facility from facsimile prints or the *Time* mats.

Thus the ease with which periodicals now can be whisked across national borders opens up a prospect of lively competition in this field. What barriers are the enterprising publishers likely to encounter? And how seriously should we take them?

One may eliminate the normal problems that beset foreign-owned business in any country: taxes, licensing, labor troubles, the complicated mechanics of nonpostal distribution which sometimes even in this country involve the payment of premiums to handlers and dealers, local laws requiring the hiring of a certain percentage of natives, and the like. Publishers have somehow got around such obstacles in the past. It is possible that here and there they will be treated worse than native publishers. When that happens, the wise publisher will set up a native subsidiary, with a few prominent native leaders on its board, as Condé Nast did in Paris and London before the war; or publish in a smaller but conveniently located country where the attitude toward business is benevolent, as *Reader's Digest* is doing in Cuba.

Political action is indicated only where discrimination becomes intolerable, where governments go beyond the standards of decency and good taste in exercising arbitrary censorship, where governments attempt to obtain corporate control through what amount to confiscation proceedings, or where governments flatly forbid foreign publishers to print or circulate their products. All but the last are susceptible of immediate regulation by treaty—a multilateral covenant setting the general framework and bilateral treaties dealing with details and special circumstances. It would appear that the opening-up of closed areas must be solved by the patient negotiation of bilateral agreements involving reciprocal inducements not necessarily falling within the mass-communication-field. (A whole list of provisos involving freedom of the press might be tied to Russia's request for rehabilitation loans, for example; it is even possible that such a suggestion would spread less consternation at the Kremlin than in some of the democratic chancelleries.) Diplomatic representatives will be expected, as in the past, to defend the legitimate interests of their countrymen with vigor; but it must be understood by the merchants who take their chances in foreign commerce that any consul or minister would be embarrassed by a request to protest a type of trade-protectionism that has become well-nigh universal.

The flow of books across national frontiers has followed a discernible pattern for the last century, with Britain, Germany, France, and Spain vying for leadership and the United States trailing far behind even such smaller countries as Sweden, Switzerland, and the Netherlands. (In 1941, the last year for which even round-number figures are available, the comparative gross export and re-export figures were: Germany, $35,000,000; Britain, $16,-000,000; Spain, $10,000,000; France, $9,000,000; Switzerland, $4,-500,000; Sweden, $3,500,000; the Netherlands, $3,000,000; United States, $800,000.) In general this has reflected a combination of language advantages (the Swiss, Swedes, and Dutch have worked extensively in German) and a spirit of enterprise. The Germans believed that if they bombarded school children with scientific and technical books, the children would grow up thinking of Germany as the logical supplier of the types of goods advertised therein. The British, for two centuries blessed with a virtual monopoly of the market for books originally written in English, were a little slow to see the literal truth of the Leipzig *Börsenverein*'s slogan, "Trade follows the book," but are rapidly making amends for their omission. Both British and American publishers were slow to match Spain's traditional cultural ties with Latin America and France's cultural ties with the whole literate world by launching their campaign to make English the lingua franca of the twentieth century. Indeed, it might fairly be said that American publishers were slow to see the value of book exports from any standpoint. No other satisfactory reason can be found for the fact that they allowed themselves to be maneuvered into a position with respect to reprint and translation rights which returns them less than an equitable share of the republisher's profit or for their failure to obtain United States adherence to some equitable international copyright agreement.

The explanation for the adverse reprint situation may have been at one time historically sound. In the early days of our country, we were almost wholly dependent on Europe for books. Until toward the close of the last century the number of books by American authors wanted in Europe was so small compared to the number of books by European authors wanted in America that publishers in this country readily agreed to terms that injured both them and their writers. When the tide began to change, American authors took matters into their own hands and extracted royalty arrangements from the British which made them quite independent of any action by American publishers. The publishers, in consequence, took no action, since they regarded the export business as a "2 per cent nuisance" anyway. Moved by this same spirit of indifference, American publishers for fifty-seven years have permitted the objections, first of the Typesetters Union and latterly of the radio-broadcasting industry, to keep the United States almost alone among leading nations from adhering to the Berne Convention—with the result that American publishers have lost tangible tens of thousands of dollars through the wholesale pirating, notably by the Dutch and Chinese, of books entirely without legal protection outside the United States and its possessions, and with the further result that the United States has permitted the pirating of foreign authors—a circumstance which seriously dilutes American claims to morality and a respect for culture. The Berne Convention is a model of the kind of international agreement which eliminates barriers in a whole area of mass communication. It provides simply that books copyrighted in any signatory country are protected by the copyright in all other signatory countries.

The coming of the cheap paper-bound reprint edition in this country, which has already lowered the forbidding price barrier to mass circulation of books in many countries, may make it possible for more books to flow across national borders than ever before. Aside from the restrictions imposed by different countries operating on different economies, which mean different levels of costs, there are copyright as well as sales-rights restrictions which now bar the free importation of books from one country to another. Already, Sweden and Switzerland are contending for the former German markets. France is waiting only for paper to double her exports. Backed by the British Council, a quasi-governmental body with a "book exploitation" fund of £400,000 sterling, British publishers are off to a good start, and it is rumored that they have plans for world markets. The question mark is the United States, for American publishers can hold the key to the most vexing problems: pirating (nonpayment of royalties where copyright protection is lost through technicalities or carelessness), varying royalty rates based on the selling price of the book, and difference in quality of manufacturing and in costs; and there is a question as to whether the rivalry between British and American publishers may become a dog-eat-dog struggle or a co-operative venture based on allocation of world markets. The chief bones of contention are Australia, New Zealand, and Latin America and possibly the Union of South Africa (the British are practically reconciled to seeing Canada in the American orbit). All these, in addition to the United Kingdom and Eire, to which American publishers lay no claim, together with the United States, form the best markets for English-language books and a consequent exchange of ideas and cultural products.

What appears to be indicated here is an early and amicable settlement of the Anglo-American rivalry, followed by an international copyright and reprint conference at which Britain and the United States would stand together for some formula designed to increase the flow of the books of all nations. The simplest, most forthright formula that suggests itself would involve a rule-of-thumb determination that any piece of literature would remain for a period of years (author's life plus fifty years) the joint property of the author and the original publishers, in all languages and in all countries; effective means to curb pirating; the abolition of block sales, tie-in sales, introductory discounts, and all other unfair competitive devices; establishment of the principle that any publisher has the right to place any original product in any language on any bookstall in any country, subject only to the circumstances governing native publishers—i.e., his ability to persuade the dealer to handle the book at the agreed-on price and discount; a strict limitation on the categories of books that may be sold abroad at below cost or through any other form of dealer subsidy, plus an equally strict limitation on the number of copies of any one title that may be so offered; and an agreement to confine government-inspired gifts of books to schools, libraries, and learned societies. Admittedly, this is an imposing assignment. But when one balances the importance of books as instruments of understanding against the realization that the total book export trade is measured in terms of tens of millions of dollars, it is difficult to see how the governments and publishers involved could justify a less resolute course.

INTERNATIONAL BROADCASTS

The projection across national boundaries of voice broadcasts is, as has been noted, largely a phenomenon of the thirties, although amateurs have been experimenting with short wave for two decades or more. International broadcasting does not necessarily connote direct broadcasting, as nations can exchange programs by mail, cable, radiotelegraph, or radiotelephone for rebroadcast over local facilities. Before the war, American stations concentrated on this method for reaching Latin America, leaving Germany, Britain, Russia, France, and Japan to bring direct short- or medium-wave broadcasting to a peak never approached in the Western Hemisphere.

As has been remarked, the future of international broadcasting is somewhat clouded, although it seems certain that the British, spurred by the wartime expansion of the government-operated B.B.C., will want to saturate as much as possible of the world with direct programming built around straight news, as well as commentary with the British point of view; and that Russia, France, and perhaps also the Netherlands, Belgium, Spain, and Portugal (because of their colonial or cultural ties abroad) will be extremely active in this field. Except for lack of adequate automatic relay points—the unique concern of American broadcasters—barriers to international broadcasting include the possibility that certain nations which are not particularly interested in it may seek to prevent the allocation of sufficient frequencies in the short-wave bands; the unregulated use of outlaw stations in small countries like Luxembourg or Tangier; jamming by clandestine transmitters; limitation of the manufacture or use of receiving sets capable of picking up direct short wave; and, in the field of reciprocal broadcasting, a disclination on the part of certain countries, notably our own, to allocate adequate time-periods to this type of service. *It would appear that most if not all these barriers could be leveled in time by the International Radio and other conferences presently charged with adjusting such matters—particularly if the conference machinery is brought within the framework of the United Nations Organization and thus given the authority of that body.*

MOTION-PICTURE EXPORTS

The history of the international flow of motion pictures is unique. From the end of the first World War, when earlier bids for mastery by the Swedes and later the British had subsided, until recently, the flow was almost entirely one way: from Hollywood to every habitable part of the globe. From the early 1920's until the mid-thirties, a score of countries seeking to establish their own infant industries fought Hollywood's domination without success. The most obvious government subsidy and protection could not obscure the fact that Hollywood had the most successful writers, the most skilful directors, the ablest cameramen, the best-known stars, and, because it paid the highest salaries, the best chance of picking off foreign stars as soon as they began to show promise. In vain did governments raise import duties and taxes on the operations of those distributing agencies they could reach, institute quotas which required that a certain number of homemade pictures be shown for every American import, devise elaborate fees for the dubbing-in of sound-track in the language of the country by native artists, and extend loans to their own producers. The foreign public wanted Hollywood films and was prepared to make trouble for any government that sought to shut them off altogether. Foreign exhibitors wanted full houses so they could pay their rent, and their landlords wanted the rent. As an example of how a uniquely popular product can override the stiffest protectionism, Hollywood's success was to be compared with that of the French dressmakers and perfume manufacturers.

The coming of talking pictures proved to be a turning-point. Pantomimists like Charlie Chaplin and Buster Keaton, who had been the idols of all the world, dropped from their pinnacles. The emphasis in Hollywood shifted from gesturing to fast-paced dialogue, much of it in an idiom that defied translation. Musical pictures became practicable for the first time. And for the first time Hollywood's rivals found themselves able to compete on something approaching equal terms. Who could sing German *lieder* better than a German? Who could tickle Gallic risibilities better than a Frenchman? It remained only to learn how to produce better pictures mechanically; and in the thirties British and French cameramen and directors who had been concentrating on national audiences began to switch to Hollywood's tried and true formulas to win international favor. Rising young stars like Michael Redgrave, Ralph Richardson, Googie Withers, Esmond Knight, Jean Gabin, and Michele Morgan and veterans like Raimu and Louis Jouvet turned their backs on Hollywood gold (it was the fall of France, not the lure of riches, that brought Gabin and Mlle Morgan to this country).

The result was better pictures. But the trend was established so shortly before the outbreak of war that few persons even in Hollywood realize the extent to which it is now likely to accelerate after the war. Russian and Swedish, as well as British and French, pictures are improving. Mexico has built up a thriving industry which already is giving American distributors some trouble in Latin America. There is little question that Hollywood is in for a type of competition that will make discriminatory government edicts all the more burdensome. The Department of Commerce listed fifty-eight separate legal restrictions adversely affecting Hollywood's export business at the outset of the war. Few have since been rescinded. Indeed, in the United Kingdom, France, and the Netherlands they have been added to and stiffened. The United Artists' general manager for South Africa, returning in August, 1945, from a fifty-thousand-mile tour of Africa, the Middle East, India, and China, reported that, although American films still were received enthusiastically, new and complex barriers were being raised against them. He discovered that the Russians were financing construction of theaters in several countries through "extremely lenient long-term loans" made with the condition that the theater-owners devote at least 15 per cent of their programs to Soviet pictures.

From the standpoint of promoting the circulation of motion pictures as instruments of understanding, it is difficult to see what can be done—or should be done—to arrest this righting of the balance. The effect of the present trend may very well be to give Americans and others a chance to see more British, Canadian, Swedish, French, Russian, and Latin-American films; and it could scarcely be argued that this would be a bad thing for international understanding. Moreover, the American film industry cannot boast, as can the American press associations, for example, that it leads the world in informational quality. Whatever Hollywood may say about our being admired throughout the world because we have not consciously tried to put our best foot forward in films, the consensus of Americans who lived and traveled abroad during the period between the wars seems to be that American movies have hindered more than furthered an understanding of us.[1] Finally,

[1] The war product of Hollywood seems not to have overcome these past shortcomings. Interesting in this connection is a recent comprehensive, detailed review of all of the Hollywood war films released during 1942, 1943, and 1944, by Dorothy Jones in the *Hollywood Quarterly*, written from the standpoint of their contribution at home and abroad to an understanding of the conflict. The survey comes to the conclusion that only 4 per cent of the entire output and 10 per cent of the "war" pictures themselves made any such contribution. Although Mrs. Jones found some of the best "war" pictures to be constructive in building understanding among the United Nations and in dramatizing honestly the fine job being done by American fighting men, she concluded that the bulk gave a distorted and inadequate portrayal of the enemy; failed deplorably in portraying and interpreting the roles of management and labor in winning the war; tended to ridicule, exaggerate, or sensationalize home-front problems; gave unfortunate portrayals of our fighting forces through slapstick treatment or overuse of the swashbuckling American hero conquering single-handed. Interesting, too, is a report from Teheran that

the United States is hardly in a position to lead a crusade for free trade.

The agreements reached during the summer of 1945 between J. Arthur Rank, the outstanding British film distributor and theater-owner, with various Hollywood interests may indicate a significant trend. These include the organization, with Pathe Industries, Incorporated, of Eagle Lion Films to distribute ten American and ten British films a year throughout the world; and the organization, with the Universal Pictures Corporation, of which Rank owns 20 per cent, and International Pictures, of the United World Pictures Company, which will distribute eight pictures from each country annually, for the most part the products of independent producers. Both agreements contemplate an extensive exchange of writing, producing, directing, and acting talent between the two countries; and it is possible that French producers may be drawn into what would seem to be taking the form of an international motion-picture cartel.

PRESS TREATIES

The problem of barriers to mass communication across national borders must be attacked from the national and international viewpoints, not alone that of industry. It must be attacked in a framework of reality. *The first step would appear to be to stake out an area of international agreement sufficiently specific to be meaningful, yet not so all-inclusive that some nations would decline to sign the whole because of objection to a part.*

As has been indicated, *such an area might cover guaranties of the right of all authorized telecommunications companies to operate everywhere with the same lack of discrimination as is accorded movement of the mails; guaranties of equal access at equal rates to all telecommunications and air-mail facilities; guaranties of access of accredited foreign observers to news and other information sources on an equal basis with nationals; satisfactory revision of existing copyright and reprint law and practice; and abolition of*

---

80 per cent of the Hollywood films stockpiled for postwar reissue in Iran were westerns and gangsters; the Russians gave Iran their best.

all forms of indirect censorship. It might also cover guaranties against arbitrary expulsion; a pledge that all governments will plainly label media owned and operated by them and that they will refrain from the more flagrant forms of propaganda.[2]

The balance—abolition of direct censorship; abolition of discriminatory taxes, tariffs, quotas, and fees; and guaranties of the right of any authorized dealer in mass media to buy and sell without interference from his government—might for the present better be left to bilateral treaties.

[2] The existing international law of propaganda forms a starting-point from which both multilateral and bilateral treaties can proceed. It is accepted as law, although a "law" flagrantly violated in pre-war international radio broadcasting, that the government of a sovereign state is bound to refrain from spreading propaganda hostile to a foreign country in that country during times of peace. International law is not so settled as to the responsibility of a government with respect to private propaganda activity proceeding from its territory. Lawyers of nineteenth-century European Continental states and more recently in Latin America have attempted to establish governmental responsibility for private propaganda similar to that established for the acts of government. Anglo-American legal opinion and practice, however, have sharply restricted responsibility over private persons and groups to the prevention of organized acts of force in the form of military expeditions and plots for assassination of political figures in a foreign country. Beyond that, these governments recognize no international law creating governmental responsibility with respect to private propaganda activities proceeding from their territory. Such responsibility, however, is at times voluntarily assumed by reciprocal provisions in bilateral treaties. The line between governmental and private propaganda activity is broadly defined so as to include under "government" organizations and agencies receiving governmental subsidy or assistance.

5

THE HARDEST JOB—QUALITY

ABUNDANT, cheap, and rapid physical communication facilities throughout the world seem possible of achievement within a reasonably short period. The elimination of barriers to the gathering, transmission, and distribution of news and information is a piecemeal process which can proceed steadily and slowly within a general framework of agreement in principle. The improvement in the accuracy, the faithful representative character, and general over-all quality of the words and images in the international market is the longest, the hardest, and the most complex task of the three—but no less important for its difficulty.

The yardstick of mass-media adequacy in international communication will not be that applied to the domestic fields in any given country; for, as has been noted, the alternative checks and balances are much fewer in international communication. If Syrian newspapers are able to get only 2,000 words a day from American press associations (as compared with an average of more than 100,000 printed daily in a New York newspaper), 2,000 from the French agency A.F.P., 5,000 from Reuter, and about the same from the official Soviet agency, Tass, Syrian newspaper readers will learn all too little about the outside world—and get even less with which to compare and check it: an occasional magazine, an even rarer translated book, the movies, and, as matters now stand, perhaps not even the few minutes of news daily by short-wave radio which the State Department has been furnishing as a carry-over from O.W.I., plus the not very far-reaching personal contacts of Syrians abroad and of foreigners in Syria.

Whatever resolutions are passed at a forthcoming World Free

Press Conference scheduled to be held in Australia, it must be borne in mind that the habit of uncovering facts and of reporting them as fully as possible and the approach to political neutrality which has come to be known as "objectivity" have been fostered only by Americans and Britons, together with certain others like the Swedes, Dutch, and Swiss, who are not likely to contribute more than a small leaven to the mass of world news. This puts an added burden upon British and American news purveyors, who must accept the grave responsibility for telling, faithfully and fully, not only the story of the English-speaking world but the story of the whole world to the whole world.

There is every indication that Reuter and the American press associations realize this and are preparing to meet the challenge. The sins of omission and commission of which they will have to repent if they are to attain adequate goals include limited distribution, insufficient volume, unrepresentative selection of items, and an almost unconscious nationalistic bias.

It would appear that the first two can be removed very quickly by turning to the maximum use of multiple-address wireless newscasting facilities for the distribution of news and news pictures. The British have discovered that the preparation and distribution of upward of fifty thousand words daily to more than three thousand newspaper customers in every part of the world is actually less expensive than Reuter's pre-war point-to-point service to some three hundred metropolitan cities. The French and Russians already have inaugurated similar services, and it is to be hoped that A.P., U.P., and I.N.S. will not permit their pre-war attachment to the older, more "exclusive," higher-profit-per-unit methods to stand in the way of doing their full share in the task of improving understanding among peoples.

Clearly, a major ingredient of universal understanding is a large volume of news moving from all countries to all countries and giving the poorest editor several tens of thousands of words daily from which to choose. It has been said that this would have the effect of submerging the editor in too much news. The argument is not impressive. No editor paying a flat rate for daily coverage ever complained of too much. Moreover, part of the job of the news purveyors is to inform editors; it does not follow, therefore, that everything editors are obliged to leave out of their newspapers is altogether wasted.

The alternatives to speedy universal adoption of the multiple-address technique seem obvious: either one or two countries will retain the initiative and thus dominate the world news market, or—what is even more likely—editors will turn to voice broadcasts for their news. The old-fashioned cable news cartel has disappeared; a radio news cartel could spring up within the next few years—but only if its victims stubbornly refused to see the handwriting so plainly written on the wall. The rapid decentralization of radio broadcasting through the springing-up of tens of thousands of F.M. stations all over the world, as well as the development of multiple-address newscasting, suggest an altogether new press-association technique designed to serve these two markets, perhaps jointly. It seems reasonable to suppose that if the existing press associations do not furnish this technique, new companies will be formed to do so. Certainly news-hungry editors are not going to overlook the possibilities of short wave simply because the board of directors of this or that press association does not like it.

THE PROBLEM OF SELECTION

The problem of selection also is one for the news purveyors themselves to solve. In the past the chief criticism has been leveled at a discernible tendency to superficiality and sensationalism. Paradoxically, press-association executives who insist upon full, cross-sectional foreign reporting for their domestic readers have sometimes excused lower standards for the export field on the ground that their customers abroad want sensationalism and triviality. Given adequate volume, *the answer to this problem would appear to be simply a matter of wise selection by competent, well-paid press-association editors familiar with the peculiar needs of various areas.*

The point has been made that no amount of objective reporting will supply all the background and interpretation required for intelligent comprehension of events in one country by the people of another. This is an extremely important point, but it should not lead to the assumption that the press associations should expand their services too much in these directions. Indeed, press-association executives are to be commended for resisting the suggestion that they interpret as well as present facts. The tradition of refraining from interpretation in unsigned news reports has been ground into English-speaking press-association reporters, particularly Americans. There is very real danger that the correspondent who was permitted to interpret would lose sight of his first task. Moreover, even if the same set of correspondents and editors were suited to the two quite dissimilar techniques, those who buy news are entitled to a clearly labeled distinction between them.

The task of supplying background and interpretive material would seem to fall to supplementary news and feature syndicates of the type that handle political and other columnists. There are syndicates such as N.A.N.A. and Overseas News Agency providing interpretive news of other countries for the American press. Unfortunately, there exists no American syndicate which distributes interpretive columns written especially for foreign audiences—for the obvious reason that no columnists write for such audiences. The O.W.I. developed a group of writers (Walter Millis, of the *New York Herald Tribune;* Barnet Nover, of the *Washington Post;* and others) who contributed special columns specifically addressed to foreign audiences. These writers soon discovered that the task required a special technique, not easy to master and, of course, completely beyond the reach of those with no intimate knowledge of foreign groups. Their only payment was the satisfaction of knowing that their efforts were regarded by hundreds of editors abroad as being among the most important contributions to international understanding.

What appears to be clearly indicated here is an altogether new type of syndicate. Based upon the growing exchange of material between pairs and small groups of newspapers in different countries, such a syndicate might operate somewhat as follows: Each of a score of newspapers in half as many countries might assign one or more well-qualified writers to interpret one domestic issue a week for foreign readers; the twenty or more resulting articles could then be exchanged within a space of seventy-two hours or less by air mail, at no cost other than the postage, plus the expenses of perhaps one syndicate manager who would visit each member-paper annually to receive suggestions and offer encouragement to the writers; the member-papers could run the exchange articles through the week or display them in a certain space in the Sunday editions. It is to be hoped that, whether or not one or more such syndicates come into being, newspapers will continue the present trend toward the exchange, as between one paper and another, of this type of material.

Governments will have a certain inevitable function in supplying various types of background material of service to editors. Care should be taken that such material is plainly labeled a government product, so that editors will be able to distinguish it readily from the commercial news product. The expressed fear of all government material presumes a naïveté on the part of the editors that does not appear to be warranted. In the final analysis they will judge everything by its degree of accuracy and lack of bias.

LIMITATIONS OF "PACKAGED" INFORMATION

In the main the social impact of printed newspapers and magazines will be limited to the extent that they are available in the language of the countries in which they are sold and to the extent that they are aimed at foreigners rather than expatriate nationals of the country of origin. The sixty-odd years' experience of the *New York Herald Tribune*'s Paris edition indicates that a periodical which appeals to one group holds little interest for the other, regardless of language. The "*Paris Herald*" could have been developed into almost a semiofficial "Voice of America," eagerly sought after in all the chancelleries of Europe; but the pre-war management elected instead to cater to American tourists, and it would appear that in reviving the paper after the liberation of France, the target is still the American abroad, although he is now being furnished a newspaper similar in scope and quality to the New

York edition. On the other hand, *Reader's Digest*'s policy of simply translating articles bought for the domestic edition could be more harmful than helpful. As has been noted, foreigners do not have access to the alternative checks and balances which the writer, addressing a domestic audience, takes for granted; consequently, domestic issues lifted out of their context and couched in the local idiom are likely to confuse and mislead the foreign reader.

It seems clear that no publication can hope to achieve permanent financial success in a foreign country unless it is sold on a mass-distribution basis, which, of course, involves printing in the language of each area—in some instances more than one language to a country. There is evidence that many countries will resist the intrusion of foreign publications. This wariness appears to stem in part from a surfeit of government-inspired propaganda periodicals; but there is also the factor of competition with local business: a superior *Life,* in French, could put *L'Illustration* on the rocks. Moreover, many persons may resent the ostentation of anything obviously more expensive than they themselves can turn out.

Whatever the plans of publishers, the usefulness of periodicals would appear, therefore, to lie in other directions—i.e., genuinely international publications and genuinely national publications designed, purely as a by-product function, to inform those foreigners who can read the language and understand the idiom.

International "digest" magazines which would serve as syntheses of useful articles drawn from many national magazines would be particularly valuable. So also would international magazines of opinion, to which writers of all nations would contribute. It is not known whether either type could ever become self-sustaining, but both recommend themselves to those foundations which have money to give away, much of it specifically earmarked for the furtherance and preservation of world peace.

On the other hand, a wider circulation of the better existing newspapers and magazines in itself would be helpful. The chief problem here is to make them available to those who, for financial and other reasons, cannot be reached by subscription sales. The almost total absence of free lending libraries and reading-rooms outside the United States complicates the problem. In the past, colleges and learned societies have provided certain of these facilities. Most governments either are using or expect to use their diplomatic missions for such purposes. But neither colleges, private libraries, nor embassies seem to attract the type of reader hitherto unreached; the premises are usually both forbidding and inaccessible.

It has been suggested that business groups maintaining offices abroad pool their resources to erect centers in the principal foreign cities, after the manner of the British Empire Building and the Maison Française in Rockefeller Center, New York City. *Such buildings could easily provide library and reading-room facilities, and foreign magazines and newspapers to fill their racks could be supplied gratis by the publishers.* This step alone might go far to correct the emphasis typified by a pre-war ratio of two hundred *True Confessions* to every *Harper's* available abroad.

The same device would be useful in making foreign books available to those who cannot afford to buy them and in the wider dissemination of books which foreign publishers do not choose to bring out as commercial risks. Books, as O.W.I., O.I.A.A., and the British M.O.I. long ago discovered, are among the most powerful instruments for improving understanding. However, the freer flow of books across national frontiers depends not only upon solution of the copyright and reprint tangles already noted but also upon the choices of local publishers, who not infrequently select the most superficial and sensational titles from the lists of foreign publishers.

THE BOOK PUBLISHERS' PLAN

During the war, book publishers got around these restraints sufficiently to publish cheap editions of useful books for distribution by governments. The average publication cost of such books was less than the equivalent of 10 cents. The British Council distributed several hundred thousand. American publishers co-operated with the Army and Navy in circulating tens of thousands of "Armed Forces Editions," and with O.W.I. in distributing thousands of "Overseas Editions" to foreign civilians.

Largely as a result of its reassuring experience with the government, the American book industry recently organized the United States International Book Association, a nonprofit, nonexclusive, federated organization set up to cope with problems in the export market. *Several members of U.S.I.B.A. have suggested that the principle of "Overseas Editions" might be extended to include all nations desiring to participate, with a view to making useful books, selected deliberately for the purpose of informing, more widely available throughout the world. The plan would operate somewhat as follows: A distinguished jury in each participating country would select each year from the titles of its publishers certain books calculated to project a people abroad; the publisher's associations like U.S.I.B.A. would arrange to print quantities of these titles at cost, in the language of the country of origin in each case; dealers would agree to retail single volumes or sets in this "Know Your Neighbor" series at cost-plus-handling—possibly not more than 10 or 15 cents a copy. Admittedly, this plan sounds utopian; but for the immediate future the publishers of each country might at least make several hundred free copies of certain of their titles available to stock the libraries housed in diplomatic missions, and also those in business centers, if the latter materialize.*

This need for functional co-operation, with each other and with government, in the export market has occurred to the private owners of mass media in most countries. In the United States, only the motion-picture industry has shown signs of following the book publishers' example. As has been remarked, Hollywood has a special problem: how to hold its initial advantage in the world market against the growing competition of foreign studios bidding not only for their own domestic markets but for a larger share in the global profits. It is becoming obvious to American producers that greater care will have to be taken in selecting films for the foreign screen—as poor pictures would tend to underline unfavorable comparison with better foreign pictures. American motion-picture distributors are organizing one or more export corporations under the terms of the Webb-Pomerene Act; but it is not yet clear how these bodies expect to control the selection of films. The plan adopted in some cases for pooling revenues from all pictures provides an excellent base for building a policy of balanced and representative selection of films in each year for each area.

Meantime, from the standpoint of increasing understanding among peoples, the problem for motion-picture producers everywhere is much more than merely selecting the best that they produce and getting their governments to batter down the artificial barriers that prevent its being shown abroad. Many of the commercial, or so-called "theatrical," movies made to date in all countries have had the effect of spreading misinformation rather than information. The British, Russian, and American governments found it necessary during the war to fill in the gaps thus created with so-called "documentaries" and specially edited newsreels. In no country but the United States has the government shown signs of retiring from this field. *A No. 1 priority for Hollywood, therefore, would seem to be to discover ways and means of taking over the documentary field.* With the example of other countries constantly before them, the American people may not be content to see their own outdone.

Robert Riskin, Frank Capra, and others who have been in government service during the war have learned that documentaries need not be dull. Indeed, anyone who has seen such pictures as *The True Glory, Fighting Lady,* and *Next of Kin* would be inclined to agree. They have done well at the box office. In the view of many Hollywood independents who intend to experiment with them, there is a wide field for these theatrical documentary shorts. But it seems likely that the industry as a whole will have to back this relatively new type of film, at least on the distribution end. Riskin has suggested that *all producers purchase stock in a nonprofit corporation to propagate documentaries and other experimental ventures for the domestic as well as the international market.*

The campaign for better short subjects, including newsreels, is not intended to deflect major motion-picture producers throughout the world from their original and primary task of entertaining. On the contrary, those who, like Riskin, argue most passionately for more "educational" shorts realize as fully as anyone in the industry that the finest documentaries will not attract maximum crowds to the theaters and are therefore relying on better feature pictures to perform that historic function. What the "reformers" are trying to say is that the industry should produce fine entertainment that does not distort current history and fine history that does not put the customers to sleep—all for the same billing.

The theatrical documentary may gain its place in the movie-house booking. The nontheatrical (16-mm.) documentary in other countries, such as Britain and Canada, has already built large audiences outside the entertainment "palaces"—in schools, lodges, churches, grange halls. *Here again is a large area for our own national production and international exchange.*

Of all the mass media, none needs functional federation more than international short-wave broadcasting; and no international broadcasters are so desperately in need of it as those in the United States. Although every other country's powerful short-wave transmitters, under government supervision and in most cases government operation, are preparing to continue or even expand present services, potential private broadcasters in the United States face a long period of uncertainty unless some solution to their dilemma is found by July, 1946, at the very latest. As has been noted, the broadcasters and a special government subcommittee wrestled with this problem throughout all of 1944 and well into 1945 without finding a satisfactory answer. Meantime, O.W.I. and O.I.A.A. have been abolished. The powerful relay stations they used to reach Europe and Africa are being dismantled or returned to their foreign owners, and operations are continuing tentatively and, since January, without benefit of A.P. and U.P. wire service until Congress, the State Department, and the industry decide what, if anything, will be taken over as part of a permanent information program.

A PLAN FOR SHORT WAVE

The most promising suggestion for postwar international broadcasting from the United States is based upon the following assumptions, supported by experience and a careful canvass of present potentialities: (1) that the maintenance of an adequate program of international broadcasts from the United States, at least for the next few years, perhaps permanently, need not be so extensive as that necessary for wartime overseas propaganda needs—perhaps 40–50 per cent of the 1944–45 O.W.I. and O.I.A.A. expenditures for short-wave voice programming; (2) that advertising of a proper and dignified kind suitable for international broadcasts will not readily support even so moderate a total expenditure; (3) that the present advertising-commercial control of programming in the domestic field is quite unsuitable in the international field; (4) that the scarcity of frequencies available for short-wave voice broadcasting and the complex scheduling of facilities necessary for sending programs to groups in different parts of the world, in different time zones, and with varying listening habits dictates operation of American short-wave voice broadcasts under a single control and unified plan; (5) that either government subsidy of an entity operating in the public interest or full government operation and programming is necessary; (6) that subsidy, not involving specific program control, to an organization of existing private broadcasters, subject to its own responsible central control of program and policy and with periodic review of operations in the public interest as a condition of relicense, would most adequately meet the requirements for financing, for program quality, for political independence, and for the public interest, provided the organization were properly managed.

Based on these premises, *the plan calls for the immediate formation by all those American companies interested in international voice broadcasting of a nonprofit, nonexclusive, federated association similar to the U.S.I.B.A.; the voluntary adoption by all the members of the federation of a code of standards covering program material and advertising; the selection by its board of directors of a chief executive of the federation from outside the industry's ranks and with an established record for public spirit, integrity, and knowledge of foreign affairs, clothed with full authority for allocating program time to the constituent companies and for enforcing strict compliance with the code.*

On the assumption that the government will operate some of the physical telecommunications facilities from the United States, the plan would provide government subsidy in the form of low rental of physical facilities. Provision would be made for government-originated programs in much the same way that government programs appear on the domestic radio, except that the low rentals might be considered payment for government programs.

Government censorship of individual scripts or programs would be prohibited by statute, as with the domestic radio at present. The individual companies comprising the federation would, however, be subject to periodic license renewal by the F.C.C.; and there would be definite provision for general review of the performance of each licensee and its compliance with the federation code and the other regulations required in domestic licensing.

Much of the success of this non-profit federation of international broadcasters operating in the public interest depends upon the ability and authority of the chief executive chosen to regulate programs and policy. He would need to be a person of courage and independence. By informal contacts with the State Department he would be able to keep the international programs reasonably in line with American foreign policy without being subservient to immediate or partisan controls. State Department objections to specific programs would be considered by him as a responsible official, but an official legally and financially independent of the government.

A trial of this form of responsible, co-operative management is well worth making. If, during a normal license period, it does not succeed, the only alternative would seem to be direct government programming and management of all international broadcasts.

The chief advantage of this plan lies in the approximate halving of nonrecoverable expense through a bookkeeping separation of programming cost from the cost of operating the transmitters and assignment of the latter to the government as a fair charge for the broadcasting of such government-originated programs as are deemed to be essential to the national interest.

A detailed analysis of O.W.I.'s international voice-broadcasting operations for the fiscal year 1945 indicates that the burden would not be excessive for either. Exclusive of transmitter charges, O.W.I. spent $27.64 per fifteen-minute program, or $2,342,190 for the twelve months' total of 84,741 quarter-hours in twenty-two languages. Transmitter costs were $39.50 per quarter-hour, or $3,336,569.50.[1]

It is estimated by some in the broadcasting industry familiar with these widely extended wartime propaganda operations that 40,000 quarter-hours would be quite adequate for normal peacetime operations. With a considerable percentage of the programs selected from high-quality domestic programs suitable for foreign consumption, as was done with such signal success in the case of the Raymond Swing Saturday night broadcasts for British listeners, the total programming cost could be brought down to something like $1,200,000 a year.

Nor would that part of the expense to be borne by the government be as large as some pessimists have indicated. It is recognized that O.W.I.'s engineering costs were abnormally high. (Private broadcasters operated for less before O.W.I. took over.) If the government operated international voice transmitters as part of an over-all telecommunications service including multiple-address newscasting, the cost of operating the facilities could, it is estimated, be brought down to $20 per quarter-hour, or something like $800,000 a year. And it should be remembered that this would not be a net figure, since the government from the outset would be earning revenue from its newscasting facilities.

Thus the international broadcasting entity could operate for one to two million dollars a year. If the federation included as constituent companies not only the present seven international broadcast licensees (C.B.S., N.B.C., Westinghouse, General Electric,

[1] Since their manuscript went to press the authors have had an opportunity to review the proposed international voice-broadcasting program of the State Department and are impressed by the case made for a much larger budget. Estimates from the broadcasters themselves run as high as twenty-five million. State originally asked for eight and one-half. The discrepancy between such figures and the authors' may be accounted for by failure of the O.W.I. officials who supplied the latter to include operations conducted during the war by the O.I.A. and by the National Broadcasting Company and the Columbia Broadcasting System under government contract.

Crosley [now the Aviation Corporation], World Wide and Associated Broadcasters, Incorporated) but also the Mutual, Associated, and American networks, possibly the Cowles Brothers and Marshall Field interests and others, the cost to be met by any one company would average $100,000 a year.

THE ROLE OF U.N.O.

The need for (1) a permanent international council, (2) an appellate body to which those working in the mass-communications media might appeal cases of unwarranted government restrictions or unfair competitive practices, and (3) an international press secretariat was recognized at the close of the first World War. The Information Section of the League of Nations Secretariat, in addition to facilitating the work of accredited correspondents in Geneva, attempted on a number of occasions to bring newspapermen together to discuss common problems and to suggest solutions for them. Through action of the League Assembly, an International Conference of Press Experts was held in Geneva in 1927 and a second conference in 1932. The Danish government sponsored an international conference of press representatives in the latter year (1932), and the Spanish government sponsored a similar meeting in 1933–34.

These conferences dealt with the problem of discrimination and high cost of telecommunications facilities generally and succeeded in lowering the cost of press transmissions to and from Geneva. They discussed government censorships, pirating of copyrighted press material, and problems of free access of reporters to news sources. On all these points there was a consensus of judgment but no decisive accomplishment. There was also prolonged consideration of the problems of the spread of false and inaccurate information and distortion of facts, with the recurrent suggestion of a journalists' court of honor to deal with specific cases. In this area there was sharp division of opinion, the United States representatives actively opposing any attempts to set up such agencies of press supervision. The emphasis in many of the resolutions on the *effect* of false information rather than on the *fact* of falsity—i.e., "news or articles calculated to cause undesirable misunderstandings among nations and suspicions detrimental to international peace"—led to opposition on the part of more than one country devoted to a free press. Foreign correspondents from democratic countries had had vivid memories of such phraseology's being used by undemocratic regimes to suppress honest, critical opinion. In any case, there was no real progress toward acceptance of codes or machinery looking toward responsibility for accuracy in reporting.

The emergence of the totalitarian governments after 1934 and the gradual decline in the League's general prestige brought an end to the conferences and any international consideration of a free and responsible reporting of information across national borders.

But the problems continue to exist. And just as the failure of the League did not deter us from setting up the United Nations as its successor, so the League's failure to solve the problems of the mass-communication media does not obscure the continuing urgency of the problems or the wisdom of renewed attempts to deal with them.

On pages 52–55 of this report there is described the International Telecommunications Union, already in existence and with definite plans for continuance and enlargement. Whether it maintains a separate existence or becomes one of the units attached to the Economic and Social Council of the United Nations, it is the proper body to deal with the whole subject of physical telecommunications facilities.

A vigorous, well-supported department of information at U.N.O. headquarters to provide full press and other information facilities is an obvious need and has been officially proposed. There remains the need for a permanent international agency, functioning as an autonomous part of the United Nations Organization, to deal with the mass-communications problems of censorship, discrimination, access to news sources, investigation of deliberate falsehoods, and encouragement of all means of improving the quality and accuracy of mass communication across national borders. Even if progress is made in framing and adopting multilateral and bilateral treaties dealing with these matters, an international unit is desirable to watch their observance and defects, to suggest revision, and to review charges of their violation.

The form of such an organization is clear enough: (1) a periodic conference of representatives of the mass-communication industries and government in each member-country, (2) a continuing executive council or board, (3) a secretariat, and (4) panels or judicial groups to review and publish findings on matters of censorship and discrimination referred to them by organized correspondents' corps in the various news centers.

Initiative in the formation of such a unit must come from the newspaper, press-association, radio, motion-picture, magazine, and book industries in the major countries. This undoubtedly will be no easy task in countries such as the United States, where national representatives of these industries have scarcely, if ever, sat down together in a single room and would still look under the bed for trouble if called together by the Department of State. But sooner or later they will see themselves as an essential segment of the organization of an international community.

A step toward organizing such a unit has already been taken on paper. Article II (2) of the draft constitution of the Educational and Cultural Unit of the United Nations Economic and Social Council states its function in part as that of assisting "the free flow of ideas and information among the peoples of the world through schools, universities and other educational and research institutions, libraries, *publications and the press, the radio and the motion picture* [italics ours], international conferences and the exchange of students, teachers and all other representatives of educational and cultural life. . . . ." But this does not represent any joint plan or project as between school, university, press, radio, and movie leaders. It expresses the initiative of scholars and educators in this and other countries. Their inclusion of press, radio, and motion pictures in their orbit was merely filling a vacuum.

What is plainly indicated is a separate mass-communications unit, distinctly above the trade-association level, co-ordinated with the Educational and Cultural Unit, or possibly with the Commission on Human Rights, and attached in the same way to the Economic and Social Council; or two or three co-ordinate sections, one dealing with education, another with mass communication, possibly a third with research and scholarship, as parts of an educational, cultural, and mass-communications unit in which the top leadership would be shared between the three professional groups.

Knowing the practical difficulties of getting the movie moguls, radio-network chiefs, newspaper, magazine, and book publishers into a common organization even on a national scale, it would seem more immediately feasible to organize the mass-communication groups into an autonomous unit under the Economic and Social Council, but with definite liaison relations to the Educational and Cultural Unit. It must be staffed with men who can bring to their task professional skill and experience, consummate tact, and the respect and confidence of those with whom they must work. The initiation of the mass-communications unit should be provided by the United States. Its beginnings are overdue.

THE NEED FOR PLANNING

The case for intra-industry co-operation in the export field has been made on the very good ground that only by uniting can the individual companies involved hope to achieve maximum success for their programs. Where government is the sole owner or dominant partner, as, for example, in Russia and France, this unity already exists. In Britain, where government operates the radio and private industry is given a fairly free hand in all the other mass media, the latter has taken the initiative in seeking unity of purpose among its members and with government. In the United States, as we have seen, only the book and the motion-picture industries have taken the first preliminary steps toward co-operation. The international broadcasters, who have even greater need for functional union, have not found it. The newspaper and magazine industries, deeply committed to laissez faire competition, have not sought and apparently do not desire federation.

Notwithstanding the obvious functional benefits of export federation—common merchandising and distributing facilities, a single voice in negotiations, and the like—they do not constitute the only motives for co-operation. Whether they welcome it or not, those who engage in the export of mass-communication media have come to be regarded as adjuncts of diplomacy and national policy. This inevitable relationship is no less real in the United States for having been avoided by government, resisted by industry, and needlessly confused by imaginary threats of encroachment upon the First Amendment.

It is obvious that both the international and the national programs for removing barriers and improving volume and quality of mass communications flowing across national borders will require prolonged study, discussion, and, eventually, some formal organization both by government and by the industries.

Thus far there have been general resolutions favoring world freedom of information passed by conventions of newspaper editors and adopted by the national political party conventions and by both houses of Congress; an equally general resolution adopted by the diplomatic representatives of the Americas at Mexico City and proposed by a group of citizens at the suggestion of the Civil Liberties Union for adoption at the San Francisco Conference, which, although it produced no general official action, was welcomed by the American Secretary of State and referred as an appropriate subject for consideration to the Commission on Human Rights brought into being at San Francisco. A committee of United States newspaper editors has toured foreign countries to gain support for the same desirable but vague objectives and has produced an optimistic account of its encounters with foreign statesmen and the press leaders. Australian editors are planning an international free-press conference. Congress has engaged in no special study of the problems. As yet no positive, specific plans have been announced or comprehensive conferences proposed to bring together the leaders of the motion-picture, radio, newspaper, book, and magazine industries with interested government officials. *Planning in this area, to be effective, must be carried on at the very highest executive, congressional, and industry levels. Positive, powerful leadership is needed in (1) the development of export federations, (2) exact drafts of treaties, and (3) consideration of the proper American initiative in helping to create a unit attached to U.N.E.S.C.O. or to the Economic and Social Council in the United Nations Organization.*

THE IMMEDIATE PROSPECTS

The State Department, commissioned by the President to outline a permanent peacetime information program for submission to Congress, soon found itself in a cul-de-sac, thanks to a number of factors but chiefly to the failure of the interested parties in government and industry to progress, in the ten months following V-E Day, beyond the resolutions stage.

The blueprint worked out by Assistant Secretary Benton, based, in part, on suggestions of Professor Arthur Macmahon of Columbia University and made public in a letter of December 31, 1945, from Secretary Byrnes to President Truman, envisioned an extremely modest program calling for "the maintenance of American libraries of information abroad; the supplying of documentary and background material by wireless and by mail to our missions overseas; the scoring of documentary films into foreign languages; the continued publication of a Russian-language magazine for distribution in the Soviet Union; the continuing supply of visual materials about the United States; the maintenance in sixty-two countries of small staffs to conduct our informational and cultural relations; [stimulation of] the exchange of students, scholars, and technicians on behalf of twenty-six agencies in the federal government; continuance of short-wave broadcasting on a reduced scale until recommendations can be made to you and to the Congress for the ultimate disposition of the transmitters and the frequencies now in the government's hands."

Unfortunately, the more urgent task of carrying on certain minimal operations of O.W.I. and O.I.A.A. that had been dumped in Benton's lap was used as a weapon to attack his long-range plans, the A.P. and U.P. excusing their summary rupture of wire service to the department with the statement that government dissemination of news handicapped them in selling their own reports abroad. The fact that A.P. sells news to Tass raises a question as to the validity of the statement. The fact that both A.P. and U.P. expressed willingness to sell news to private broadcasters for world-wide dissemination by short wave suggests that some or all of the short-wave licensees, having failed in three years to produce a workable plan for continuing this vital service under other than government auspices, but nonetheless eager to get hold of the transmitters and frequencies, welcomed such action by A.P. and U.P. as a way to accomplish this. The fact that A.P. and U.P. regard a few hundred words of news daily as serious competition abroad, although they do not so regard the many thousands broadcast in the United States, suggests the volume of news which they themselves expect to export to those who can pay for it. Finally, the fact that all that was involved in their dispute with Benton was continuation of service to the State Department from February 1, when it was cut off, to July 1, by which time Congress will have accepted, modified, or rejected Benton's long-range plans, strongly suggests that, despite the particularization of the indictment, the press associations and broadcasters are opposed to Benton's entire program and are anxious to get back to a situation in which not only foreign editors but our own diplomatic representatives were completely dependent on private agencies for news from America.

One need not be committed to the doctrine that governments have an inescapable responsibility to disseminate informational material to recognize that the immediate prospects are not encouraging. The authors happen to believe that it would be far better for all concerned if private agencies assumed the full responsibility for improving understanding among peoples everywhere to the extent that the media of mass communication can accomplish this. Without exception, the private agencies in this country have said that they would do this. The fact is that, as of February, 1946, they were not doing it. The authors believe that the acid test of good faith, in so far as the press associations are concerned, is their willingness to exploit multiple-address newscasting to the extent that Reuter, no less jealous of government interference, has exploited it for four years. They find it difficult to reconcile the A.P.'s and U.P.'s promises to the American people with the fact that, three months after its offer of world-wide multiple-address press facilities at one-third of a cent a word, the Mackay company had no takers.

The hour is late. But even now there is still time for co-operation between private industry and government in the United States, based on a thorough working knowledge of the facts and personalities involved rather than on hearsay and threadbare slogans. It must be obvious to the directors of mass media everywhere that there are functions and activities vital to increasing understanding among peoples which private industry cannot undertake on the basis of normal commercial incentives. It must be equally obvious to them that the alternatives are two: either they must discover new ways to cover these neglected areas, or governments ultimately will have to step in and do the job; for, inevitably, the people who elect governments will one day want to see the job done.

6

PROPOSALS

A NUMBER of specific proposals by the authors designed to carry out each of the Commission's general recommendations (pp. v–vii) are submitted in the paragraphs that follow.

1. To secure THE IMPROVEMENT OF PHYSICAL FACILITIES AND OPERATING MECHANISMS SO AS TO BRING ABOUT THE COMMUNICATION OF WORDS AND IMAGES ACROSS NATIONAL BORDERS AS ABUNDANTLY, AS CHEAPLY, AS QUICKLY, AS EFFICIENTLY, AND OVER AS WIDE AN AREA AS POSSIBLE, the following proposals are addressed to Congress, the Department of State, and the Federal Communications Commission: That

   a) All United States cable and radiotelegraph companies, with exceptions to be noted below, be merged, voluntarily if possible (and if not possible, by congressional act) and joined with government facilities not needed after the war for military purposes, to establish a global telecommunications network to handle commercial, military, diplomatic, press, and voice-broadcasting traffic.

   b) Exemption from the merger be allowed for a single telecommunications corporation devoted entirely to the transmission of press matter, provided that such corporation maintain membership rules to provide inclusion of all bona fide press-users, including newspapers, press associations, magazines, and radio-broadcasting companies, and with voting arrangements calculated to distribute control fairly among these different users; and that if no such telecommunications corporation applies for the privilege of exemption, there be made specific regulations in the merged corporation for autonomous physical and financial operation of press-transmission facilities.

c) Exemption from compulsory merger be granted for the present also to existing radiotelephone facilities.

d) In the organization of the merged corporation, definite provision be made for a revaluation of the cable company investments so that their valuation will be in close relation to present actual capital value.

e) Definite provision for regulation of the merged corporation in the public interest be made either by government ownership of a majority of the stock in the merged company, with consequent majority membership on the board of directors and with statutory limitation of dividends of the stock privately held in the merged corporation; or by private ownership of all stock in the merged corporation with specific power of comprehensive regulation of rates and services, including extension of service in the public interest, assigned to the federal regulatory authority.

f) By government control of policy or by governmental regulation as defined above, positive steps be taken to provide physical facilities for multiple-address dot-dash, and facsimile (including radiophoto) wireless transmission and direct international voice broadcasting, so that these facilities, together with facilities separately furnished by the press-facilities corporation, will cover every habitable part of the world.

g) Definite arrangements be completed at an early date for acquiring automatic relay stations for multiple-address newscasts and short-wave voice broadcasts from the United States to Europe, Africa, and Asia, for the use of United States public or private corporations authorized to carry on such services.

h) The United States become a full member of the International Telecommunications Union and participate actively in efforts (1) to establish adequate registration, monitoring, and adjudication machinery to bring into full force the maintenance of an orderly observance of international frequencies assigned for all purposes on the channels appropriate for long-distance telecommunication; (2) to establish bilateral agreements in the commercial cable, radiotelegraph, and radiotelephone fields designed to reduce rates and to eliminate discrimination as between people of different countries and as between sparsely settled and thickly settled parts of the world, to promote direct access and direct circuits and to foster, where applicable, the uniform-rate principle; (3) to consider the development of international machinery for the most economical and co-operative organization of international voice broadcasting and multiple-address press transmission, including the possibility of setting up powerful regional transmitters for general use under the United Nations machinery; (4) to encourage the development of an international broadcast station serving directly as an instrument of communication to nations of the world from the committees and councils composing the United Nations Organization.

i) The United States become a full member and participate actively in inter-American telecommunications conferences and conventions looking toward the same objectives.

2. To secure THE PROGRESSIVE REMOVAL OF POLITICAL BARRIERS AND THE LESSENING OF ECONOMIC RESTRICTIONS WHICH IMPEDE THE FREE FLOW OF INFORMATION ACROSS NATIONAL BORDERS, the following specific proposals are addressed to Congress, the Department of State, and the appropriate representatives of the other United Nations: That

a) There be incorporated, within the framework of United Nations agreements, a multilateral covenant stating that the signatory nations believe in, and will do their utmost to bring about, the fullest possible flow across national borders of true information concerning all events and peoples.

b) Specific sections of such a covenant include the following provisions:

(1) Guaranty of equality of access to the sources of information as between co-nationals and foreigners;

(2) The organization in all principal news centers of the world of foreign correspondents' corps with strict, self-administered codes of ethics; the requirement that all newspaper, magazine, and radio reporters and all authors and photographers (including newsreel cameramen) be members of these corps and bound by their codes; specific authority for the corps to handle all disputes among members or with host-governments, with right of appeal to a unit of the United Nations Economic and Social Council previously described;

(3) Guaranty that no country will expel a member of the foreign correspondents' corps or interfere with his normal activities pending final recommendation in such cases by the unit of the United Nations Economic and Social Council, on the advice of the correspondents' corps involved;

(4) Guaranty that the signatory nations will keep correspondents faithfully informed of such rules of censorship as are in force; that they will adhere strictly to these rules at all times; and that, as far as possible, they will limit them to open deletion or suppression in the presence of the author;

(5) A pledge that all governments will plainly label and identify all media owned and/or operated by them and all products issued by them in international communication;

(6) Guaranty that no country will practice arbitrary and unreasonable discrimination against foreign periodicals seeking to gain access to legitimate markets within its borders;

(7) Similar guaranties covering radio programs and motion pictures;

(8) As regards books in international communication, acceptance of the principle that any piece of literature

will remain for a period of fifty years or more the property of the author and original publisher, in all languages and in all countries; effective means to curb pirating; abolition of block sales, tie-in sales, introductory discounts, and other unfair competitive devices; acceptance of the principle that any publisher has the right to place any original book in any language on any bookstall in any country, subject only to the conditions governing co-national publishers—i.e., his ability to persuade the dealer to handle the book at the agreed-upon price and discount; a strict limitation on the categories of books that may be sold abroad at less than cost or through any other form of dealer subsidy, and an equally strict limitation on the number of copies of any one title that may be so offered; and agreement to confine government-inspired gifts of books to schools, libraries, and learned societies;

(9) The creation of an autonomous unit in the United Nations Economic and Social Council, and co-ordinated closely with the United Nation's Educational, Scientific, and Cultural Organization (U.N.E.S.C.O.) or with the Commission on Human Rights, to promote the free flow of true information and the removal of artificial barriers restricting such free flow. This unit, among other things, (*a*) to scrutinize the observance of the provisions of the multilateral treaty described above, to suggest changes in it from time to time, and to publish its findings and recommendations for the information of the United Nations Assembly; (*b*) to assist in the formation of professional foreign correspondents' corps as described above; (*c*) to receive, to consider carefully, and to report on individual or collective violations of the multilateral treaty; and (*d*) to investigate (by aid of monitoring of broadcasts, examination of printed material, and pictures) areas in which distortion of facts and fomenting of international discord are being car-

ried on, and to report to the Assembly on such dangers to peace and understanding.

The following specific proposals are submitted to Congress and the State Department: That

a) The United States seek, through the negotiation of bilateral, reciprocal treaties with as many nations as possible, to achieve the following:

(1) Abolition of direct censorship;

(2) Abolition of unreasonably discriminatory taxes, tariffs, import quotas, fees, and unreasonably discriminatory exhibition and publication practices calculated to exclude the informational, cultural, and entertainment products of either of the signatory countries from the other;

(3) Guaranty for any authorized press association, newspaper, news-picture agency, syndicate, magazine, book publisher, writer, radio station, or motion-picture studio of one country of the right to sell its product directly to any individual newspaper, radio station, motion-picture exhibitor, magazine, book publisher, or dealer in the other country.

b) The United States adhere to a world copyright convention.

3. To secure THE IMPROVEMENT OF THE ACCURACY, REPRESENTATIVE CHARACTER, AND QUALITY OF THE WORDS AND IMAGES TRANSMITTED IN INTERNATIONAL COMMUNICATION, the following proposals are addressed to the appropriate leaders of private industry in the United States: That

a) There be set up, immediately, federated, nonprofit, co-operative associations, with nonexclusive membership, in each of the following industries: newspapers, magazines, books, radio, and motion pictures, similar to the United States International Book Association. Each of these associations to have as its functions:

(1) Assurance of means by which the best domestic products are distributed in foreign countries at prices and in amounts calculated to assure wide audiences;

(2) Discouragement by self-regulatory agreement of the export of substandard American products;
(3) Encouragement and creation of products such as documentary films and magazine digests, especially designed to present a truthful picture of American life;
(4) Joint study of areas abroad not reached by existing means of distribution on a profitable basis and encouragement of nonprofit organizations, foundations, or governmental units to serve such areas;

b) In the field of international voice broadcasting, where the usual competitive commercial activity is not profitable, technically feasible, or proper, there be set up such a federated, nonprofit association of all broadcasting companies desiring to participate, with the following special arrangements:
(1) Use of physical facilities as provided above for shortwave broadcasting under license, as now domestic radio is licensed by the Federal Communications Commission;
(2) Choice by the association directorate of a chief executive selected from outside the industry, with full authority for allocating program time to constituent companies and for regulation of all program material and advertising copy to comply with strict standards defined by the association;
(3) Prohibition, as now in domestic radio, of any government censorship of individual programs; but with review by the Federal Communications Commission, as now in domestic radio, in connection with application for renewal of individual licenses, of each licensee's general performance in the public interest.
(4) Should the broadcasting companies not succeed in organizing and financing an association within the terms of the proposal here described, as determined by the licensing agency, and should no other private group so qualify, steps should be taken to organize a government

unit to undertake the function of international voice broadcasting.

4. We propose to the Congress that the State Department be authorized to adopt as its frame of reference for future operations in the cultural and informational fields the following broad principles: That
   a) It continue to operate any and all services formerly operated by the Office of War Information and the Office of Inter-American Affairs which have been demonstrated to be valuable for the promotion of international information and understanding and which private industry cannot or will not undertake;
   b) It develop immediately, with competent and professionally trained personnel, its foreign information attachés to be of the greatest service to the private information agencies here and abroad and assist in every possible way in the coordination and encouragement of all activities designed to promote the full and free exchange of true information among peoples.
5. We propose to the appropriate leaders of private industry in the United States and to the State Department that, in order to facilitate the orderly division of responsibilities thus clearly indicated, they meet together immediately to formulate an integrated program designed to achieve the maximum objectives as described above and set up a standing industry-government committee to develop and perpetuate such a program.

NOTE ON SOURCES

BOOKS AND BOOKLETS

There is no general treatise on international mass communication or any recent, thoroughgoing study of telecommunications, press associations, books and copyright, radio or motion pictures, separately. A volume entitled *Telecommunications* by James Herring and Gerald Gross (the latter for several years a chief of the International Division of the Federal Communications Commission) gives a comprehensive account of the development of that field up to the time of its publication (1936), but much of significance has occurred in the last decade. A British publication (1944) of the Royal Institute of International Affairs, *International Telecommunications,* by Brigadier General Sir Osborne Mance, fills in the more recent picture, as well as giving a concise account of early developments in international negotiation and conference in this area. Kent Cooper's *Barriers Down* gives a readable, autobiographical account of the world cartel of press associations and Associated Press's involvements in it and later extrication from it. But the equally interesting account of the pioneering of the United Press in foreign countries is not in print—and has been made available to us only in an oral, personal account by Karl Bickel, U.P.'s ex-chief. An informative little booklet telling the story of American efforts in the field of international communication in and around the Paris Peace Conference (1918) has been published by the Columbia University School of Journalism in the *Annual Report* of the Dean for the academic year ending June 30, 1943. Various articles and speeches by Chairman James L. Fly during and since his tenure as chairman of the Federal Communications Commission, dealing vigorously with various aspects of the general problem, have appeared in the last two years, the most comprehensive of which is being published by the University of Chicago as part of the proceedings of the Twenty-first Institute of the Norman Wait Harris Memorial Foundation, July, 1945, with the title *Freedom of Communications.* A recent booklet (1945) issued by the American Newspaper Publishers Association and prepared by Louis Caldwell, entitled *The American Press and International Communication,* has valuable material based on Caldwell's extensive experience as attorney for communications industries and service as chief counsel of the Federal Radio Commission. The report of the World Free Press Committee of the American Society of Newspaper Editors has been useful in underlining the obvious difficulties in the way of achieving world freedom of press communication. *Unwritten Treaty,* by James P. Warburg, is a plea for international regulation of propaganda, as well as a useful history of its development from the rise of Hitler. The Memorandum on the Postwar International Information Program of the United States by Dr. Arthur W. Macmahon, published by the Department of State (1945) is a very valuable analysis in this area.

PUBLIC DOCUMENTS

Of government documents especially to be noted are the testimony at the hearings (still far from concluded) before the (Wheeler) Senate Subcommittee of the Committee on Interstate Commerce (69th Cong., 1st sess.); mimeographed documents issued in connection with the extensive Federal Communications Commission hearings in the fall and winter of 1944–45 on the problem of frequency allocations in the whole radio spectrum, including reports issued by the Interdepartmental Radio Advisory Committee (I.R.A.C.) and Radio Technical Planning Board; British P.E.P. reports dealing with such subjects as postwar information services; and, from an earlier period, the British Parliamentary Committee's testimony with regard to Cable and Wireless, Limited. Accounts of the various conferences and agencies in the field of international telecommunications are to be found in the *Journal des Télécommunications,* issued monthly by the Bureau of the International Telecommunications Union located at Berne; of European activities especially, in the monthly *Bulletin of the International Broadcasting Union* located at Geneva (before the recent war); and of Pan-American activities, in the *Bulletins* of the Pan American Union.

MEMORANDA

Of more value in connection with the present study have been a number of typewritten memoranda; minutes of agency, departmental, and interdepartmental committee meetings; staff memoranda and reports, circulated in the State Department, Office of War Information, Federal Communications Commission, Office of Inter-American Affairs, and Bureau of the Budget—also memoranda circulated by Press Wireless, Incorporated, which the authors have been allowed to examine but which, for obvious reasons, are not subject to specific quotation. Ralph Nafziger, of the University of Minnesota School of Journalism, prepared for the staff of the Commission on Freedom of the Press a valuable account of the League of Nations activities in the field of international communications.

INTERVIEWS AND CONFERENCES

The largest part of the experience, facts, and ideas summarized in the report, however, come from interviews by the authors together or singly and from conferences by members of the Commission, in groups or as a whole, with officials in the mass-communications industries and in government.

The report itself, in four successive drafts, has been discussed in detail at meetings of the Commission on Freedom of the Press over the period of a year; and the origin of many of its paragraphs can be traced to the suggestions and comments of Commission members in oral discussion or in written memoranda circulated between meetings.

Over a period covering more than a quarter-century, the authors, other members of the Commission staff, members of the Commission, and advisers have talked with several hundred experts in the field of international communication.

At the top political level these would include the heads of state and cabinet ministers in the United States, the United Kingdom, Canada, Australia, France, Belgium, Brazil, Venezuela, Mexico, Denmark, and China; members of Congress and the parliaments of the United Kingdom, Canada, Australia, France, Belgium, and Brazil; officials of the Department of State, the British and French Foreign Offices, the Bureau of the Budget, the Federal Communications Commission, the Interdepartmental Radio Advisory Committee, the Office of War Information, the Office of Inter-American Affairs, the United States Army and Navy, the British Ministry of Information, the British Council, and the French Ministry of Information.

Also interviewed were the top executives of the Associated Press, the United Press Associations, International News Service, Reuter, Havas, Tass, Agence France Presse, the Central News Agency of China, Tidningarnas Telegrambyraa of Sweden, and others; the *New York Times*, the *New York Herald Tribune*, the *Christian Science Monitor*, the *Chicago Tribune*, the *Chicago Daily News*, the *Chicago Sun*, the *Portland Oregonian*, the *Minneapolis Journal and Tribune*, the *Des Moines Register and Tribune*, the *Louisville Courier-Journal and Times*, the *Detroit Free Press*, the *St. Petersburg Times*, *La Prensa* of Buenos Aires, *Paris-Soir*, the *London Daily Express*, the *Wiener Neue Freie Presse*, the American Newspaper Publishers Association, the American Society of Newspaper Editors, and the British Newspaper Proprietors Association, as well as *Time*, *Life*, *Fortune*, the *Saturday Evening Post*, *Collier's*, the

American Magazine, This Week, Reader's Digest, Newsweek, and *Harper's.*

Other organizations with the members of which the Commission has discussed the question are the following: the Columbia Broadcasting System, the National Broadcasting Company, the American Broadcasting Company, the Mutual Broadcasting System, the General Electric Company, the Westinghouse Company, the Crosley Corporation, the World Wide Broadcasting Foundation, the British Broadcasting Corporation; the Hays (Johnston) Office, Twentieth Century–Fox, and other motion-picture concerns; Reynal and Hitchcock, D. Van Nostrand, the Macmillan Company, Simon and Schuster, Harper and Brothers, Pocket Books, Inc., the Council on Books in Wartime, the United States International Book Association; Cable and Wireless, Limited, the British Post Office, Western Union–Postal Telegraph, the International Telephone and Telegraph Company, the American Telephone and Telegraph Company, Press Wireless, Incorporated, and R.C.A. Communications.

DIRECT OBSERVATION AND EXPERIENCE

The authors have also drawn directly on experience in the field of international mass communication in preparing the report. Mr. White's experience includes service as assistant managing editor of the *New York Herald* (Paris); day copy chief of the *New York Herald Tribune;* New York wire editor for Associated Press; Paris correspondent for United Press; assistant managing editor of the *Literary Digest;* national affairs editor and radio round-table moderator for *Newsweek;* editor of the editorial pages and Washington correspondent of the *Chicago Sun.*

During the war just ended, Mr. White was chief of the News and Features Bureau of the Overseas Branch, Office of War Information, an outgoing press service from the United States to foreign countries. This service included a point-to-point and multiple-address press transmission of more than 125,000 words daily, in addition to pictures, mats, and feature stories. From Office of War Information field stations in foreign countries he obtained a firsthand picture of the operating problems, uses, and actual demand for such services. For several months just previous to his joining the staff of the Commission he served as special advisor to the director of the Office of War Information, working exclusively on postwar problems related to the international exchange of information.

Mr. Leigh during the recent war was director of the Foreign Broadcast Intelligence Service of the Federal Communications Commission and chairman of the United Nations Monitoring Committee. This service operated monitoring posts at favorable points along the American coasts, in island possessions, and later in conquered territory; and had teletype, cable, facsimile, or air-mail connection with English, Australian, Canadian, and Dutch monitoring posts by means of which enemy radio broadcasts of whatever origin and destination were recorded and the valuable information contained in them (intelligence) furnished on a twenty-four-hour ticker-service basis to all the United Nations information, diplomatic, and intelligence services. In effect, this operation was a world-wide press association, but with material selected entirely as important fact rather than for its "news" value and serving only government agencies. It provided unusual opportunity to make continuous, detailed comparison of news with intelligence.

The Commission was particularly fortunate in having the close counsel of Archibald MacLeish during the final preparation of this Report. An original member of the Commission and chairman of its Committee on International Communication, Mr. MacLeish was obliged to interrupt his earlier labors to become Assistant Secretary of State in charge of information and cultural relations, an experience the lessons of which he has been able to bring back to the Commission.

SUMMARY

This report, therefore, is compounded in varying proportions from five sources: books, public documents, interviews and conferences, Commission discussions, and direct experience in the field.

PUBLICATIONS OF THE COMMISSION

The general report of the Commission on Freedom of the Press will appear during the present year (1946) at the termination of the Commission's work. In addition, special studies under the authorship of individual Commission members, or members of the staff, will be published. The first of these is the present report in the field of international communication, prepared by Llewellyn White, assistant director, and Robert D. Leigh, director, of the Commission's staff.

Other special studies now being prepared for publication are the following (subjects rather than exact titles are given here):

1. *Freedom of the Press—a Framework of Principle for the Twentieth Century.* By William Ernest Hocking, professor of philosophy, emeritus, Harvard University.

A re-examination of the classic foundation of freedom of the press in philosophy and law in the light of the immense technological advance in instruments of communication, the vastly increased requirements of free communities today for reliable service of news and opinion, and the extreme power which the agencies of communication now wield.

As freedom of speech and of the press are ingredients of our picture of a free society, the general nature of freedom in the modern state is first examined, both as a value and as a right. It is pointed out with special emphasis that the notion of rights, which had a militant value in the eighteenth century, requires revision; there are no unconditional rights; every right has its corresponding duties and its assumptions regarding the purpose of the claimant; every right may be forfeited or limited if the conditions are not met.

These principles are then applied to the right of free expression in speech and press. This is followed by an examination of the implied, but hitherto almost unrecognized, right involved in the free press, especially in its news service—the right of the public to be served with a substantial and honest factual basis for its social judgments. Although the press in this respect assumes an essential public service and thus incurs a just public concern for the quality of its performance, so that the laissez faire principle must be rejected, the author points out the strong presumption against governmental intervention whether to perform or to regulate this service. He defines four fields of proper governmental activity, shows that the degree of freedom from the touch of government must vary with conditions of public temper, and urges the assumption by private agencies and by the press itself of a greater measure of initiative and responsibility for the quality of the output of press, radio, film, and other agencies of communication.

Various members of the Commission, in appended notes, have carried on discussions with the author of points where divergence of viewpoint on specific sections of the analysis exists.

2. *Government and Mass Communication.* By ZECHARIAH CHAFEE, JR., professor of law, Harvard University—with a section on "Government as a Party to Communication," by the Hon. JOHN GRIERSON, formerly general manager, Wartime Information Board, Canada.

An extensive analysis of the threefold relation of government to mass communication: (1) the use of governmental power to limit or to suppress discussion, (2) affirmative governmental action to encourage better and more extensive communication, and (3) government as a party to communication.

The volume covers the whole field of governmental and legal regulation of the press under peacetime conditions, with special attention to certain areas where proposals are currently made to alter existing statutory, judicial, or administrative practice. These include libel and compulsory correction of published errors, post-office mail-exclusion orders and denial of second-class privileges, compulsory disclosure of source, laws requiring collective bargaining, and anti-trust statutes as applied to the press industries. The author's recommendation regarding many of these problems is included.

A special section reviewing the war experience with regard to government as a dispenser of information at home and abroad, with an analysis of the desirable scope of this function in time of peace, is included.

3. *The American Radio.* By LLEWELLYN WHITE, assistant director of the Commission on Freedom of the Press.

A story of radio's first quarter-century—its amazing physical growth, its economic and artistic development, its attempt to regulate itself, the government's attempt to regulate it, the consumer's attitude toward it. The author applies to the broadcasting industry the yardstick of accountability for performing an important intelligence function, defines the points of defect, and makes definite proposals for improvement which take account of the technological developments now on the way or on the horizon.

4. *Freedom for the Movies.* By RUTH A. INGLIS, research staff, Commission on Freedom of the Press, formerly of the Smith College department of sociology.

An analysis of the forces which restrict the content of films and the trends which may result in a freer screen. The nature of the motion-picture industry and the mosaic of overlapping controls stemming from state and municipal censorships, federal and international restrictions, and pressure groups are described. The origin, purposes, and current operation of the producers' own self-regulation of movie content is presented in detail.

The importance of factual films is assessed—both in theaters as a supplementary part of commercial entertainment programs and outside of theaters as an adjunct to the activities of institutional and informal social groups.

The study concludes with a look toward the future, indicating the trends and probable next course of development. Recommendations are built upon an analysis of the economics and the social structure of the motion-picture industry and include practical suggestions for increasing the use of films as a vital part of the sensory equipment of the nation.

5. *The American Press and the San Francisco Conference.* By MILTON D. STEWART, with an Introduction by HAROLD D. LASSWELL, director of War Communications Research, Library of Congress.

A systematic study, on a comparative basis, of the treatment given the San Francisco Conference by the general newspaper and periodical press, press associations, radio, films, and special-group publications. The need for a positive as well as a negative conception of freedom is discussed, and six standards are proposed as an essential tool for gauging the freedom and the responsibility of the press in actual operation. This is followed by statistical summaries and examples of the levels of performance reached in covering the first U.N.O. conference by about seventy daily newspapers, forty general magazines, the four major radio networks, the five leading newsreels, and several hundred group publications. Comparisons of achievement within each medium and among the media are made.

PRINTED IN U.S.A.